Henri POUGET DE SAINT-ANDRÉ

THE HIDDEN AUTHORS of the FRENCH REVOLUTION

OMNIA VERITAS.

HENRI POUGET DE SAINT-ANDRÉ
(1858-1932)

**THE HIDDEN AUTHORS OF THE FRENCH REVOLUTION
(BASED ON UNPUBLISHED DOCUMENTS)**

*Les auteurs cachés de la Révolution Française
(d'après des documents inédits)*
1923, Librairie académique Perrin & Cie

Translated and published by Omnia Veritas Limited

*O*MNIA VERITAS.

www.omnia-veritas.com

© - Omnia Veritas Ltd - 2024

FOREWORD

In this volume I shall not attack any form of government, nor criticise any political opinion. I shall endeavour to study with impartiality the background to the French Revolution, and, in the words of the late Albert Vandal, "to present as a historian the facts that belong to history".

CHAPTER I

THE REVOLUTIONARY ENIGMA

It seems, Robespierre once said to Amar, "that we are carried away by an invisible hand beyond our control: every day the Committee of Public Safety does what it decided not to do the day before. There is a faction led to lose it, without it being able to discover the directors[1]".

The more one studies the history of the French Revolution, the more one comes up against enigmas. First of all, the writers contradict each other on most points, so that if we were to accept all their denials and rectifications, we would come to the conclusion that virtually nothing happened between 1789 and 1793! As for the rare events on which they agree, they never give the same explanation.

Why do the cahiers of the Estates General seem to have been dictated by an occult committee which substituted its ideas for those of the various French provinces?[2] Who then, asks Mr L. Madelin,[3] after having had the cahiers drawn up, paid for the

---

[1] Mémoires de MALLET DU PAN, t. II, p. 69.

[2] *Review of Historical Questions.* July 1910. Article by M. G. GAUTHEROT.

[3] *The French Revolution*: MADELIN, p. 36.

propaganda?

On the same day, who announced throughout France the arrival of imaginary brigands, a pretext for arming the people and creating a national guard?[4]

Why, after putting up with a few rather dubious sovereigns, did the French guillotine the most debonair, the one with the best intentions?

It was a royalist assembly, by Mr Aulard's own admission,[5] that proclaimed the republic; no one in France called himself a republican, except an Englishman, a Prussian and a Belgian, Thomas Paine, Anacharsis Cloots and François Robert.

Was the aim of the Revolution the reform of abuses and the conquest of liberty? It should have stopped at the end of 1789. Was its aim a change of regime? It should have ended on 10 August. Why, in the words of Granier de Cassagnac[6], were the reforms that Louis XVI offered for nothing bought at the price of four billion and fifty thousand heads?

Why did the Convention shed so much blood? It has been said that the proscriptions were caused by the hatred of the people for the privileged classes. How then to explain the low proportion of aristocrats guillotined, around 5% of all those condemned?

The presidents of the Convention can be considered to be the most immune to proscription, since they represented the majority of the proscribers. They were, as the saying goes, on the side of the stick. What explanation can be given for their fate: eighteen were guillotined, eight deported, six imprisoned, twenty-two

---

[4] *Mémoires de Mme de la Tour du Pin*, p. 191. *Mémoires de Pasquier*, etc.

[5] AULARD: *Histoire politique de la Révolution Française*, p. 87 and p. 175.

[6] Cassagnac: *Causes of the French Revolution.*

outlawed, three committed suicide and four went mad![7]

All the people of France are against us," Robespierre said from the rostrum of the Jacobin Club. Our only hope lies with the citizens of Paris. —Don't put too much faith in that," replied Desfieux, "even in Paris we would have the upper hand if the ballot were secret[8]".

Where does Robespierre's ascendancy over men who were superior to him in talent and intelligence come from? Michelet, who is not among the reactionary historians, observes that Robespierre was a small lawyer of mediocre figure, mediocre intelligence and colourless talent.

"As Mr G. Lebon says at[9], "We can explain a tyrant surrounded by an army, but not the tyranny of a man without soldiers.

The party that drove the Revolution to violence "was directed by a hidden hand that time has so far been unable to make known"[10].

Bailly, also taking up Robespierre's idea, wrote in his Mémoires[11] that as soon as the Bastille was taken, there was "an invisible engine that conveniently sowed false news to perpetuate unrest. This engine must have had a large number of agents, and to have followed this abominable plan, you need a profound mind and a lot of money. One day we'll find out who the infernal

---

[7] TAINE: La Révolution Française, t. III, p. 222.

[8] Buchez et Roux: Histoire Parlementaire, t. XX, p. 300. Sybel: Histoire de l'Europe, t. 1, p. 564.

[9] La Révolution Française, G. LEBON, p. 231.

[10] Alexis Dumesnil: Preface to the Mémoires de Sénar.

[11] Mémoires de Bailly, tome II, p. 33.

genius was and who provided the funds.

Finally, Lafayette also wrote on 24 July 1789: "An invisible hand directs the rabble".

"The closer we have come to the instruments and actors of this catastrophe, the more obscurity and mystery we have found; this will only increase with time[12].

Simple minds were content with Etienne Dumont's explanation: "The cause of the Revolution is the weakness of Louis XVI. It is also too easy to attribute events to the influence of the devil, as J. de Maistre did; for men who study history seriously, there is something else. Disraëli, a highly intelligent Jew who occupied a prominent place in English politics, admitted: "The world is governed by quite different characters than those who are not behind the scenes imagine[13]". But he was careful not to name the hidden leaders of politics. The learned work of Mr G. Bord has given a very curious and well-documented explanation of events: the Revolution was due to a Masonic plot[14].

There is certainly a lot of truth in this assertion; but then we come up against another enigma: if the Revolution was made by Freemasonry, why were the lodges closed in 1793 and above all why were so many Freemasons guillotined?

But let's look at the hypothesis of the Masonic Revolution.

---

[12] *Mémorial de Ste-Hélène.* t. II, p. 82.

[13] DE LANNOY: *La Révolution préparée par la franc-maçonnerie*, p. 14.

[14] Gustave Bord: *The Masonic plot of* 1789.

CHAPTER II

THE FREEMASONS

The Freemasons, no doubt through an excess of modesty, have always denied having been the authors of the French Revolution. Their political opponents have often been treated as fantasists who attribute murky activities to a charitable society; but when they are sheltered from profane ears, the language of Freemasons is no longer the same. Bro. Sicard de Plauzoles had just stated at the 1913 convent: "Freemasonry can with legitimate pride consider the Revolution as its work[15]. At the 1910 convent, Br. Jouvin also spoke of the Masonic action of 1789, which was also affirmed by Br. Louis Blanc in his history of the French Revolution.

But it was above all the International Masonic Congress of 1889 that provided interesting details on this subject. On the occasion of the centenary of our Revolution, Br. Amiable and Colfavru read out two well-documented reports to the Grand Orient on 16 July, summarised below:

"At the beginning of 1789, the Freemasons took an active part in the great and salutary movement which took place in the country. Their influence was preponderant in the assemblies of the Third Estate, for the drafting of the cahiers and for the choice of elected representatives... They had a less considerable role in

---

[15] TOURMENTIN *Freemasonry unmasked.* 10 March 1911.

the assemblies of the two privileged orders. However, the influence of Freemasonry can still be seen in the numerous reform proposals in the cahiers of the nobility and the clergy...

The Freemasons penetrated the National Assembly in large numbers and, to show the place they occupied from the outset, we need only name three of them: Lafayette, Mirabeau and Sieyès[16].

... The plan for the Encyclopédie had been drawn up eleven years in advance by Freemasonry...

The National Assembly had moved on from programmes and wishes expressed in notebooks after being prepared in the lodges. In 1789, the great French Masonic family was in full bloom. It had received Voltaire in the famous Lodge of the Nine Sisters, presided over by Lalande. It knew Condorcet, Danton, Robespierre, Camille Desmoulins... The most illustrious would found the new social and political edifice on these luminous principles: Liberty, Equality, Fraternity. But by the time they had accomplished their sublime task, they would all be dead...

In 1792, the Freemasons had to devote themselves to fulfilling their ever-increasing civic duties: service in the National Guard, military service, the incessant work of the popular societies to support the National Assembly, to foil the manoeuvres of the officials of the old regime who had not yet been replaced, repeated elections, mandates taken up and functions exercised at all levels in the commune, the district, the department and the State. This is why the Masonic temples, gradually deserted, remained empty.

After a general assembly in December 1792, the Grand Orient

---

[16] Minutes of the sessions of the International Masonic Congress of 1889. Report by Fr. Amiable, p. 68 ff.

ceased to function in the middle of 1793. A very small number of isolated lodges were able to continue their work. It was an eclipse of almost three years[17].

It is regrettable that these documents do not provide an explanation for the question we posed at the beginning of this volume: how was such a powerful association unable to stem the revolutionary torrent and oppose the proscription of the most illustrious Masons?

The Masonic action of 1789, ignored by so many historians, is not a recent discovery, since as early as 1792, Le Franc wrote: "All that we have seen carried out by the clubs had been prepared at length in the Masonic lodges[18]". Le Franc's revelations were also the cause of his death sentence.

Like the clubs, Freemasonry is an English import[19]; the first lodge was established around 1725 in Paris by a number of Englishmen, the most notable of whom was Lord Derwent Waters, who was later beheaded in England for having taken up arms in favour of the pretender Charles Edward. In 1736, Lord Harnouester was elected Grand Master by the four lodges of Paris and was succeeded by the Duke of Antin. Already under Louis XV, the internationalist doctrines of Masonry were beginning to make themselves known: one is surprised to read the following sentence in a speech by the Grand Master in 1760: "The whole world is but one great republic of which each nation is a family. It was to spread these essential maxims that our society was first established."

One hundred and fifty years later, this is exactly the

---

[17] Report by F.—. Colfavru to the 1889 congress.

[18] N. Le Franc: *Conjuring against the Catholic religion and sovereigns*.

[19] According to César Moreau's *Précis sur la Franc-maçonnerie*, the existence of this secret society in England dates back to the end of the third century.

conclusion of Br. Amiable's report to the 1889 Congress: "A universal and democratic republic is the ideal of Freemasonry".

In every age, a programme of universal peace and brotherhood must appeal to many men with excellent intentions. But the events of 1914 have just shown how dangerous it is to give in to pacifist dreams, suggested by a neighbour who is silently arming himself.

After the closure of the Grand Lodge of France in 1767, a number of workshops continued to meet; some lodges were under the jurisdiction of the Grand Lodge of England or other foreign powers [20] . The table of Masonic Lodges in the correspondence of the Grand Orient de France in 1789 shows four Scottish Directory Lodges and six provincial Grand Lodges, including one in Friedrichstein in Westphalia. In all, there were 629 lodges, 63 of which were in Paris, 442 in the provinces, 38 in the colonies, 69 attached to military corps and 17 in foreign countries.

Thus, England had not ceased to exert its influence on French Freemasonry; we shall return to this important detail later.

Under Louis XVI, Freemasonry had made rapid progress in France and was gradually preparing for a change of regime. Fr. Amiable was therefore right to conclude in his report to the 1889 congress: "The Freemasons of the eighteenth century brought about the French Revolution".

The privileged orders had merged with the Third Estate in the lodges before doing so in Versailles. Officers of modest rank were seen to have as subordinates in the lodges those who commanded them in the regiment. The sergeant of the French

---

[20] Compte rendu des séances du congrès maçonnique international de 1889. p. 66.

Guards held meetings with the general officers[21]. You can guess what the result was in terms of discipline.

For example, in the "Union de Toul Artillerie" lodge, the Sergeant Compagnon, a venerable member, was the superior of Marshal de Camp d'Havrincourt[22]. The greatest lords and princes of the blood gradually joined the sect.

"The existence of the higher grades was carefully concealed from them; they knew only as much about Freemasonry as could be shown to them without danger". Since the sect included a large number of men "opposed to any project of social subversion, the innovators multiplied the degrees of the ladder to be climbed, creating back-lodges reserved for ardent souls[23]." It was these back rooms that prepared and directed the Revolution, while the majority of members believed they were part of a philanthropic association. While the Paris lodges were giving fetes and feasts, foreign Freemasons were actively conspiring. Weishaupt's Illuminati are planning to overthrow all monarchies. According to Gustave Bord, they do not preach the assassination of sovereigns, as they have often been accused of doing; if they did, they would inspire horror in most initiates. The sect is much more formidable when it pretends to have generous ideas. Little by little it creates a revolutionary movement of opinion and destroys people's respect for kings.

The Illuminés never entrust their letters to the post office; members of the society go from one home to another to carry and receive notices of interest to the association[24].

---

[21] Minutes of the sessions of the International Masonic Congress, p. 60.

[22] MADELIN: *La Révolution,* p. 24.

[23] Louis BLANC: *Histoire de la Révolution Française,* t. II, ch. 2.

[24] *Revue des Sociétés Secrètes,* 20 May 1913.

However, it is accepted that the death of Gustav III was a crime committed by the Illuminati. If they were suspected of other assassinations, it must be admitted that appearances were against them. Two sovereigns in Europe declared themselves hostile to the Revolution, the King of Sweden and the Emperor of Austria: the former, contrary to the advice of his ambassador, Staël Holstein, wanted to intervene in France when he was assassinated. The emperor died, it is said, as a result of his debauchery; nevertheless, one cannot help but notice that he was quite well on 19 February 1790, at the court ball, when a masked woman offered him a sweet. Twenty-four hours later he was dead.

Mirabeau siding with the king could have stopped the Revolution. As soon as the secret societies became suspicious of him, a strange incident occurred: Pellenc and Frochot, having taken coffee intended for Mirabeau, became seriously ill. When the famous tribune fell ill, he thought he had been poisoned; orders were given to say that he was dying as a result of his excesses, like the Emperor of Austria; nevertheless, seven doctors concluded that he had been poisoned: Dr Larue, Dr Chêvetel, Dr Forestier, Dr Paroisse, Dr Roudel, Dr Couad and Dr Soupé [25] . Fourcroy, a future member of the Académie des Sciences, told Cahier de Gerville that Mirabeau had succumbed to a mineral poison, and that silence was maintained in order to avoid unrest[26].

It must be admitted that chance served the revolutionary plans admirably, which explains the accusations that are impossible to prove.

---

[25] *Mémoires de Mirabeau,* t. VIII, p. 464.

[26] *La Révolution, La Terreur, Le Directoire,* by DESPATYS (based on the memoirs of A. GAILLARD, President of the Executive Directory of Seine-et-Marne).

Gustave Bord denied the crimes attributed to the Freemasons, but acknowledged that the Illuminati of Bavaria were working *"by every means possible"* to bring down monarchical governments.

Here is what Cagliostro said about his initiation into the sect: "The first blows of the conspiracy against the thrones were to reach France; after the fall of the monarchy, Rome was to be attacked". Cagliostro learned that the secret society of which he was now a member had strong roots and possessed a war chest. "He received a large sum of money, intended for propaganda costs, instructions from the sect and left for Strasbourg[27]. Two delegates, Busche and Bode, were then sent to Paris to reach agreement with the French lodges. According to Georgel's memoirs, the leaders of the sect decided to start in France because Germany was not yet ready for the Revolution. Why not also assume that our Catholic monarchy was unsympathetic to the Israelite Weishaupt? It was he who sent his co-religionist Cagliostro to prepare French Masonry to accept the leadership of the German Illuminati. It was he who tried to create an international federation of lodges[28]. At the same time, Thomas Ximenès was travelling around Europe with a mission from the sect; Cagliostro met him in a large number of cities, always under different names and disguises, spreading money everywhere.

During his trip to Berlin, Mirabeau came into contact with the Illuminati, and it is worth comparing his opinion at the time with his later conduct. Their party," he wrote, "is gaining ground in the most frightening way. I am going to reveal to you in this respect an anecdote which it is infinitely important for my safety to keep secret:"—The anecdote is replaced by full stops in the

---

[27] Louis BLANC: *La Révolution Française,* t. II, ch. 2.

[28] Report read at the plenary meeting of the Peace and Union and Free Conscience lodges at the Orient de Nantes on 23 April 1883. Dasté: *Marie Antoinette et la Révolution,* p. 194. Omnia Veritas Ltd, www.omnia-veritas.com.

various editions of Mirabeau's works; the manuscript is in the archives of the Ministry of Foreign Affairs[29].

"Two men of distinguished birth, both in the service, both still zealous Freemasons, had thought they saw in the Masonic societies some resources, one for his ambition, the other for humanity... They were destined for the highest ranks... They were initiated on the same day, one in Berlin, the other in Breslau...

The recipient is required to fast for 24 hours... then he is forced to drink a spirituous liquor, and placed in a room draped in black, lit by three yellow candles. Five men, dressed as magicians, appeared and sat down on cushions; several terrible bangs were heard, followed by groans and convulsions. A man comes up to the initiate and places on his forehead an aurora ribbon covered with silver characters; a second ribbon, marked with several crosses drawn in blood, is placed around his neck. Finally, he is given a second copper cross bearing hieroglyphs, a sort of amulet covered in cloth and a piece of alum, which he is supposed to put in his mouth when the infernal spirit that has been evoked appears...

It consisted of the promise to reveal to the head of the order any secrets that might be confided or discovered, to explore everything that it was important to know; to use iron or poison if necessary; to make fools of those whose days it was imprudent to cut short. (This part of the oath includes the words: *honora semper aquam nefariam)*. To submit any religion, any promise, any duty, any feeling to the decision of the chiefs. To give the right of death to anyone who could be convinced of having betrayed the secrets entrusted to them.

This execrable oath so horrified the proselytes that they

---

[29] Prussia: Memoirs and documents, v. 14.

declared they could not take it. These are the literally concordant details revealed by two men) reputed to be people of honour, without consulting each other or seeing each other. Let it not be said: But how are these two men still alive? Because, apart from the fact that one of them, the most shrewd, is withering away visibly, it was not under Frederick II that two distinguished officers could be made to disappear.

… This homicidal sect, which holds kings, philosophers and courageous minds under the point of the sword or poison, has leaders, ministers and regular communication. The provincial chiefs have been called to Berlin by their high priest, the ambitious Welner.

The following year, the Illuminés delegates in Paris were introduced by Mirabeau to the Amis Réunis lodge, and an alliance was concluded between French Freemasonry, the Illuminés and the Martinists. What was the reason for this about-turn by the famous orator? Probably the influence of the beautiful Henriette Herz; at all times the beauty of Jewish women has been one of the instruments of the Israelite conquest. The Mendelssohn salon, where Mirabeau met Henriette Herz, was a meeting place for the Illuminati. If we reject this hypothesis, we could still assume that a deal was struck at a time when Mirabeau needed money.

The "Amis Réunis" lodge, where Mirabeau introduced the German delegates, was specially responsible for foreign relations. Chaired by Savalète de Lange, it was run by a secret committee made up of Willermoz, Court de Gébelin, Bonneville, Mirabeau and Chappe de la Heuzière, Martinist deputy at the Willhemsbad Congress. This committee had already convened an international convent on 15 February 1885, attended by Talleyrand, Cagliostro, St-Martin, Mirabeau and St-Germain. If the minutes of these meetings could be discovered, they would undoubtedly provide the key to most of the events of the Revolution. But the reports published by the *Monde*

Maçonnique[30] have carefully suppressed anything to do with politics.

Nevertheless, they contain an important and edifying list to which we draw the attention of authors who deny the action of foreigners in the French Revolution.

The members of the Convent, most of whom took part in the votes, included:

Prince Ferdinand of Brunswick.

Prince Charles of Hesse.

Prince Louis of Hesse.

Prince Frédéric of Hesse.

General Rheinsfort (in London).

Baron de Bentz, Chancellor of Saxony.

Prince of Nassau.

Duke of Luxembourg.

Baron de Seckendorf (in Anspach).

Maubach (in London).

D'Ester (in Hamburg).

Brooks (in London).

Schmerber (in Fransfort).

Boode, alderman in Weimar.

Heseltine (in London).

The Margrave of Anspach.

---

[30] The Philalethic convent, 1785–1787. *Masonic World,* v. XIV and XV. See supporting documents.

Baron Decking (in Warsaw).

Baron de Ditfurth, Weimar.

Count d'Esterrazzi[31], in Vienna.

Deick, professor at Leipsick.

D'Haugwitz[32].

Forster.

Baron de Gleichen (in Regensburg).

Prince of Anhalt (in Hamburg).

Hemerberg (in Frankfurt).

Matolay (in Vienne).

Docteur Prévost (Galicia).

De Roskampf, alderman in Heilbronn.

Doctor Stark (in Darmstadt).

De Toll (Stockholm).

Toedon, army surgeon in Berlin.

Count Zapary (Vienna).

Count of Wachter (Frankfurt).

Comte de Stroganoff (St-Pélersbourg).

Count Wolner (Berlin).

Baron de Sibal (Stockholm).

De Bernières, Cre général des Suisses.

Kœner (in Leipsick).

---

[31] We respect the spelling of the *Masonic World.*

[32] This is obviously the adviser to the King of Prussia, whom we will talk about later.

Count of Brülh, lieutenant general in the service of Saxony…

Baron de Beulwiz (Gondelstadt-Thuringia).

De Falgera[33], (Munich), etc...

Because of this surprising number of foreign Freemasons, the following resolution was passed: "Two protocols will be held, one in German led by Br. Baron de Gleichen and the other in French led by Fr.—. de Chefdebien[34]."

Already the affair of the necklace, skilfully engineered by the lodge des Amis Réuni[35], had compromised the queen, discredited the episcopate and accentuated the rift between the court and parliament. Goethe suggested that this affair was "the immediate preface and foundation of the Revolution[36]. As early as 1786, Cagliostro predicted the destruction of the Bastille and some of the events that took place three years later[37].

Little by little, Freemasonry invaded the parliaments and the entourage of Louis XVI, and founded 81 lodges in Paris and more than 200 in the provinces[38].

The parliamentarians belonged to the Strict Observance of the Reformed Templars in Germany, whose Grand Master was Duke Ferdinand of Brunswick; it was this latter grouping "that would

---

[33] The report notes that FALGERA is in Paris with "the famous Mlle Paradis".

[34] *Masonic World*, v. XIV, p. 104.

[35] DESCHAMPS: *Les sociétés secrètes*, t. II, p. 129.

[36] FUNK BRENTANO: *L'affaire du collier*, -, p. 2 ff.

[37] DE LANNOY: *La Révolution préparée par la franc-maçonnerie*, p. 39. Omnia Veritas Ltd, www.omnia-veritas.com.

[38] BARRUEL: *Mémoires sur* le *Jacobinisme*, v. p. 65.

make the first and most serious assault on the monarchy[39].

The Prussian influence on Freemasonry was not new: As early as 1762, a commission meeting in Bordeaux drew up the statutes of the Scottish rite. We know that this rite constitutes a sort of aristocracy within Freemasonry. Article 3 establishes "a Sovereign Council made up of the presidents of the particular councils, under the presidency of the Sovereign of Sovereigns, His Majesty Frederick II, King of Prussia, or his representative[40]".

Frederick II took an interest in the work of the lodges, while the Duke of Orléans only attended feasts and banquets. In 1786, a few months before his death, the King of Prussia presided in person over the Supreme Council, which increased the number of degrees in the Scottish Rite to 33[41].

The Union Lodge in Frankfurt declared that it recognised no other authority than the Grand Lodge of London[42].

Another detail indicates the agreement existing between English and Prussian masonry: On 10 February 1790 Prince Edward of England, the Duke of Kent and Prince Augustus Frederick Duke of Sussex, were received as members of a Berlin lodge[43].

The revolutionaries had discovered in the royal family an

---

[39] G. BORD: *Autour du Temple,* t. II, p. 501.

[40] Organisation in France of the 33 degrees of the Scottish rite (Le *Monde maçonnique.* v. III, p. 155).

[41] Report by Bro. PYRON.

[42] Findel: *Histoire de la franc-maçonnerie,* t. I p. 342.

[43] *Id.* in vol. II, p. 14, F.—. FINDEL moreover denies the action of Freemasonry on the French Revolution.

ambitious man willing to overthrow Louis XVI in order to take his place; this unscrupulous prince was unintelligent enough to believe that the Masonic motto L. P. D. *(Lilia pedibus destrue),* meant Louis Philippe d'Orléans. As he also possessed a magnificent fortune, he would be the ideal leader: he would be used to launch the movement, and then he would be got rid of. The Duke of Orléans was therefore appointed Grand Master of Freemasonry in 1771, on the death of Cte de Clermont. But his role was limited to appearing from time to time at ceremonial occasions[44].

At the end of 1788, two of the directors of the German Illuminati, Bode and Knigge, travelled to Paris to activate the preparations. At the opening of the Estates General, a propaganda lodge was founded at 26, rue Richelieu; the Duke of Orléans contributed 400,000 francs, and subscriptions, whose lists cannot be found, added 1,100,000 francs. Among its members were the Englishmen Boyle, O'Kard, O'Connor, Price, and William Howard, the Genoese Clavière, Duroveray and Verne, the Spaniards Benarvides, St Severanda, d'Aguilar, d'Oyoso, the German Grimm, and others. Lord Stanhope, one of the leaders of English Freemasonry, was a frequent visitor. This shows the extent to which Freemasonry seems to have been influenced by foreigners. Moreover, Cagliostro admitted during his trial that he had received the mission of preparing the French lodges to accept the leadership of the German Illuminati.

The Count of Haugwitz, one of the leaders of Prussian Masonry, confessed on leaving the sect that the French Revolution, regicide, etc., had been resolved in Germany by Freemasonry[45]. This explains the word attributed to Mirabeau; pointing to Louis XVI at the opening of the Estates General, the

---

[44] Report of the Masonic Congress of 1889, p. 52.

[45] See the article on the condemnation of Louis XVI by Freemasonry in the supporting documents.

tribune is said to have exclaimed: "Here is the victim".

It is worth noting that of the 605 deputies of the Third Estate, 477 belonged to Freemasonry.

After 17 June 1789," wrote Judge Colliette Mégret to Interior Minister François, "you would have thought you were in a lodge at the National Assembly. Freemasonry made a prodigious contribution to the Revolution[46]. "Mégret reported the revival of Freemasonry in Germinal An VII: "The lodges seem to be rebuilt on all sides. Only tried and tested citizens are accepted because of their hatred of royalty and anarchy, and their attachment to the republic and the Constitution of Year III. Any member who varies in this respect will be expelled and proscribed".

In short, Freemasonry has been a marvellous instrument of demolition; but it seems to have been employed by the invisible hand of which Robespierre speaks. The impetus seems to have come from Germany and England. Once the monarchy was overthrown, the power of Freemasonry declined, at the precise moment when foreigners no longer needed its services. During the Terror, the main lodges closed and many of the sect's leaders were proscribed. It was not until 1795 that Rœltier de Montaleau set about reviving the lodges. The first major celebration organised in Paris by 18 lodges took place in 1797. F.—. Colfavru noted at[47] that "under the sinister man of Brumaire, masonry developed... but it could only live by flattering the despot". It will continue to make protestations of devotion and loyalty to the Empire, the Restoration, Louis Philippe, Napoléon III, etc., and we can say with F.—. Colfavru: "Nothing is more wretched than these adulations, these sycophancies of

---

[46] Archives nationales. F^7 7566 R^1 630.

[47] Report to the International Masonic Congress of 1789.

power[48]."

People who do not want to admit the Anglo-Prussian leadership of Freemasonry in 1789, can explain the role of the sect by the ancient Templar tradition: since the death of Jacque Molay, the Templars have always planned to take revenge on the King of France and the Pope. M. Tourmentin, the famous anti-Mason writer, has collected a number of curious documents on the Templar origins of Freemasonry. On the other hand, Bro. Jouaust [49] denies this hypothesis and provides fairly good arguments in favour of a purely English origin.

Be that as it may, the English influence and even the Prussian influence during the revolutionary period seem indisputable.

After the fall of the monarchy, it was German Illuminism that launched the idea of the Feast of the Goddess Reason and proposed a new religion, destined to supplant Catholicism. Next, it is almost impossible to discover the relations of our Freemasonry with other countries. We need only recall a very accurate observation by F.—. Dequaire at the 1889 Congress: "The great movement of 1789 is unintelligible to anyone who has not prepared to study it with the help of Masonic history".

Henri Martin rightly called the secret societies "the laboratory of the Revolution".

---

[48] *Id*, p. 75.

[49] *Le Monde Maçonnique*, v. VI, p. 9.

CHAPTER III

THE ISRAELITES[50]

I s Freemasonry currently run by the leaders of the Israelite nation? Many authors affirm this, but evidence is lacking. In principle, Jews are not part of the Order's Council. However, in 1886 Brother Hubert wrote in the *Chaîne d'Union, the* journal of universal masonry: "At all times we have accepted Israelites into our Masonic workshops… The list would be long if I wanted to undertake to enumerate the names—among the most remarkable—of Israelites who have been or are still part of Freemasonry"[51].

Bernard Lazare claims that there were Jews at the cradle of Freemasonry[52].

Later, a Freemason told M. de Camille: "I left my lodge because I became convinced that we were merely the instrument of the Jews"[53].

At present, about twenty per cent of the members of English

---

[50] In order to avoid rectifications, we call Jews not only those who practise the Jewish religion, but all people who belong to the Israelite *race.*

[51] See *Revue des Société Secrètes,* 1918.

[52] Bernard Lazare: *Antisemitism, its history, its causes.*

[53] Delassus: *La question juive*, p. 20.

Freemasonry are Israelites: 43,000 out of 225,000[54]. The Hiram Lodge is entirely Jewish.

In Prussia, on the other hand, the main lodges did not admit Israelites.

In the eighteenth century Jews were not easily received in our lodges.

This is no longer the case and the Dreyfus Affair proved the influence exerted by the Jews on Freemasonry. It has been asked whether the Judeo-Masonic alliance existed in 1789. Here are the arguments in favour of this thesis: Weishaupt, founder of Illuminism, was an Israelite, as were Paschales and Martines, leaders of the Martinists.

The first two Freemasons to play a political role were also Jews, Cagliostro and St Germain. The two Prussians who distinguished themselves in the assault on the monarchy, Ephraim and Anacharsis Cloots, belonged to the same race. The "religious rites of all the Illuminated have borrowed from the Kabbalah"[55].

Finally, the Misraïm rite was created in France during the First Empire by a Jewish adventurer, Brother Bédarrides.

Supporters of the opposite thesis reply that while it is certain that Cloots, Ephraim and Weishaupt were Jews, there is some uncertainty about Cagliostro, Paschales, Martine and St-Germain.

The situation of the Jews in France under Louis XVI was quite inferior; the leaders of Freemasonry belonged to the Latin

---

[54] Theo. Dedalus: *Jewish England.*

[55] DELASSUS: *The problem of the present hour.*

and Anglo-Saxon races.

Be that as it may, it is curious to compare the small number of Israelites living in Paris at the time of the Revolution with the importance of the role they played. We know what their situation was under the monarchy; it is quite natural that the Jews were in favour of a change of regime. Moreover, since the secret societies attacked Catholicism, the Jews were naturally the allies of the Freemasons, and they would continue to be so under all regimes. In the words of Mr E. Flourens, "the work of demolition will not stop until the kingdom of Israel stands on the ruins of the Christian empires".

We should not forget the words of an English rabbi quoted by Sir J. Readcliff[56]: "Every war, every revolution brings closer the moment when we shall reach the supreme goal towards which we are striving". It is well known that this goal is the establishment of the supremacy of the Jewish race over the whole world.

Here is the plan set out in the minutes of the secret meetings of the wise men of Israel, concerning relations with Freemasonry: "We will multiply the Masonic lodges in all the countries of the world; they will be centralised under a single leadership known only to us and unknown to others. They will have their representative on our Board of Directors, where this representative will liaise with the Masonic government"[57].

Freemasonry has always championed Jewish claims; as early as 1781, an Israelite, Morin, was appointed Grand Inspector General of Paris Freemasonry[58]. It was in an Israelite salon, at the home of the Mendelssohn family, that Mirabeau made contact with the Illuminati, whose founder Weishaupt was Jewish. From

---

[56] *Le Contemporain.* 1er July 1880.

[57] Protocols of Israel. Edition de la vieille France, p. 54.

[58] Lecouteulx de Canteleu: *Sects and Secret Societies.*

the day Mirabeau met the beautiful Henriette Herz in this salon, he became the defender of the Israelites in France[59].

Usually absorbed in their own business, the Jews of France seemed to have nothing to do with politics under Louis XVI. The first Jews to play a role were a Sicilian, Cagliostro, and a Portuguese, St-Germain, who acted as a link between foreign Freemasonry and the French lodges.

Balsamo, the son of a banker, had left Italy to avoid conviction for forgery; he earned some money in London by blackmailing his way to Germany. There he became both a doctor and the Count of Cagliostro. When he arrived in Strasbourg in 1780, he performed marvellous cures[60], won everyone's sympathy and inspired unlimited confidence in Cardinal de Rohan. He found a way not to be too compromised in the affair of the necklace, but nevertheless he was exiled and settled in London. After several trips to Italy, Germany, Switzerland, etc., Cagliostro was condemned in Rome because of his membership of secret societies, and his eventful career ended in prison.

St-Germain was rumoured to be the natural son of the King of Portugal. In reality, we are not sure of his father's true homeland; we only believe that he was an Israelite banker, probably Portuguese. In Milan, St Germain was called the knight Valdone, in Vienna the marquis of Montferrat, in Venice the count of Bellemare, in other countries the count of Tzagory, the count Soltikof, or the knight Schœning. What's more, he spoke every

---

[59] Claudio Janet : *The Precursors. Secret Societies.*

[60] However, his treatments had one drawback: in serious cases, he could only cure the disease by sending it to another person (see Dauphin Meunier, *La Comtesse de Mirabeau*).

language, which facilitated his metamorphoses[61].

St-Germain succeeded in capturing the confidence of Louis XV and, according to M. Lenôtre, spied for Frederick II. He aroused the suspicions of the French government to such an extent that Choiseul ordered his arrest in 1759; but St-Germain escaped and took refuge in London; after the Seven Years' War he accepted the hospitality of Prince Charles of Hesse and stayed with him until his death.

St Germain wore up to 200,000 francs worth of diamonds on his clothes and, like Cagliostro, had very large sums of money at his disposal. Casanova[62] describes his introduction to St Germain as follows: "He was dressed in Armenian robes and a pointed cap. He held an ivory wand in his hand. He said to me in all seriousness: 'It's the Count of Cobentzel, Prime Minister of Austria, who is giving me work. To please him, I'm working on setting up a factory".

Casanova adds that St Germain changed a twelvepenny coin into a gold coin in front of him. It's exactly the same process as Cagliostro's: persuade fools that you possess supernatural power and, under cover of eccentricity, carry out the secret societies' missions in the shadows.

The first pamphlets against Marie Antoinette were published in London by the Jew Angelucci, who in England called himself W. Hatkinson. We shall see in Chapter VIII how the whole campaign against the Queen was organised by the Jew Ephraim. As Maria Theresa of Austria had persecuted the Israelites, it had been decided that revenge would be taken on her descendants;

---

[61] Lenôtre: *Prussiens d'hier et de toujours. L'espion sorcier du roi de Prusse*, p. 141.

[62] *Memoirs of Casanova*, vol. IV, p. 265.

the jailer Simon took charge of it.

The book by the Prussian Jew Dohm on the emancipation of the Israelites "had more influence than can be said on the opening of the Revolution"[63]. The Jew," said Bernard Lazare, "has a revolutionary spirit, whether conscious or not"[64]. The Jewish newspaper *Haschophet* recently claimed that the French Revolution was a purely Semitic work[65].

It should be noted that the encyclopaedists who launched the revolutionary movement were anti-Semitic, and Voltaire, among others, called the Jews "the most hateful and shameful of the little nations[66]". In his philosophical dictionary, he notes that they have "the most invincible hatred for the peoples who tolerate and enrich them".

But when the philosophers had turned everything upside down, the Israelites were the first to take advantage, with their usual skill.

Louis XVI had decided in 1788 that civil rights would be granted to the Israelites. He does not seem to have been grateful for this, and the Revolution took all the credit. —We find this remark in the writings of a very worthy Israelite who embraced Catholicism, Abbé J. Lémann. He also formulated the disadvantage of Louis XVI's decision with great finesse and judgement: "The Jews have always wanted to form a separate and impenetrable nation; ... to make them citizens would be to

---

[63] J. Lémann: *L'entrée des Juifs dans la société Française* p. 373.

[64] Bernard Lazare: *Antisemitism, its history, its causes.*

[65] Mgr Delassus: *La question Juive*, p. 18.

[66] *God and men.* Ch. X. Theo. Dedalus: *Jewish England.*

introduce an armed nation into a disarmed and trusting nation"[67].

Indeed, one of the great skills of the Israelites was to transform a question of race into a question of religion; in this way they were able to accuse the anti-Semites of religious intolerance, and often win the support of the Protestants against the Catholics. In the words of Portalis, they are "not so much a religion as a people that exists among all nations without merging with them"[68].

As soon as the royal decision to emancipate the Israelites was announced by Malesherbes, the Jews wasted no time in putting forward the banker Haller as a candidate for the finance portfolio. But it was still too early to defy prejudice; moreover, according to Mercy Argenteau's correspondence, Haller had the reputation of an unscrupulous agioteur.

Almost all the Israelites who played a role at the start of the Revolution arrived from abroad. Those in France, satisfied with their lot, no longer had any grounds for revolt. Nevertheless, the slogan of overthrowing the monarchy and Catholicism remained unchanged, and they followed their foreign co-religionists with the solidarity and discipline that were their strength. "During the revolutionary period, the Jews did not remain inactive," says M. B. Lazare[69]. Given their small numbers in Paris, they occupied considerable positions as section electors, legion officers or assessors, etc.". Of the 500 Parisian Israelites, one hundred were in the national guard[70].

According to M. E. Drumont, Marat was of Jewish origin; one

---

[67] J. Lémann: *L'entrée des Israélites dans la société Française*, p. 397.

[68] Denais Darnay: *The Jews in France*.

[69] Bernard Lazare: *Antisemitism in France*.

[70] Monin: *The Jews of Paris*. L. Kahn: *The Jews of Paris during the Revolution.*

of his biographers, Cabanes, also mentioned this hypothesis, which we have not been able to verify. But according to most authors, the finance minister Clavière was Jewish[71], and certainly the two Prussians who played a major role in the Revolution.

Clavière, expelled from Geneva in 1782, made his fortune on the stock exchange; a collaborator of Mirabeau and Brissot, he published the *Chronique du mois* with Condorcet; he also wrote for the *Courrier de Provence*. Clavière was a member of Freemasonry. If the Larousse dictionary is to be believed, he sold a process for preparing the Philosopher's Stone to a Masonic lodge, which involved calcining a newborn child in a retort! Larousse does not say what the industrial results were. But the Revolution soon enabled Clavière to succeed in even more fruitful operations: in charge of finance in the Dumouriez ministry in 1792, he was sacked along with Roland and returned to power after Dumouriez's departure.

Clavière has been accused of being an agent of England; in any case, he was in frequent contact with the bankers Boyd and Kerr, Pitt's agent in Paris. At the same time, he kept up an active correspondence with Bichoflswerder and Lucchesini, advisers to the King of Prussia and militant Freemasons.

Outlawed with the Girondins, Clavière was arrested on 2 June 1793. He had been administrator of a life insurance company; the liquidators prosecuted him: 1° "For theft of about four million which are in deficit in the fund. 2° For having stolen shares whose value is estimated at two to three million. 3° For fabricating documents and deliberations intended to cover up the traces of this theft"[72]. Clavière having committed suicide in prison, the trial was interrupted, but his brother was arrested as he was about to take his savings to Geneva (3 Frimaire, year 2).

---

[71] However, Mr Chuquet disagrees.

[72] Archives nationales. F. 7 4649.

This brother had just entered the ministry for foreign affairs. The file is silent on the end of his career; there is only mention of Madame Clavière's suicide two days after her husband.

The two Clavière brothers were frequently visited in prison by their co-religionist, the banker Bidermann[73].

Having settled in Pari in 1789, Bidermann was appointed treasurer of the Ministry of Foreign Affairs three years later, and chose J.-J. Clavière, the minister's brother, as his clerk. He was the speaker on a deputation sent by the Paris Commune to the Convention; shortly afterwards he took an active part in the insurrection of 10 August. When he was arrested during the Terror, his friends pointed out that Bidermann "never stopped working for the Revolution... He is Swiss; he and his whole family have always been counted among the most ardent friends of the French Revolution"[74]. The report to the Revolutionary Court notes that on the night of 9 to 10 August, Bidermann did not leave the Commune's General Council for a moment to "prepare the triumph of liberty and foil the Court's plot. It was at his request that the Pont-Neuf was cleared of the cannons that the Court had had placed there to fire on the people... In November he was chosen by Pache to be one of the directors of the subsistence commission[75], was persecuted by Dumouriez and Custines and was the first to reveal their treachery[76]". A letter from Madame Bidermann also pointed out to the Committee of Public Safety the "countless sacrifices made by her husband to contribute to the success of the Revolution", a discreet reference to the sums paid by the banker to political figures. If, as in a

---

[73] Archives nationales. W[1] 300.

[74] Archives nationales. F. 7 4598.

[75] We have described the unpatriotic role of this committee in the history of General Dumouriez (a volume published by Perrin in 1913). But personally Bidermann does not seem to have committed any wrongdoing.

[76] Archives nationales. F 7 4598.

modern trial, a financier threatened to name names, this would not be implausible. In any case, Bidermann, released on 19 Thermidor, was able to quietly resume his financial speculations.

Recent publications have shed light on the role of the Frey brothers, who married their sister to the famous Chabot, and were for a time the auxiliaries of Jean de Batz[77]. Born in Moravia, their real name was Dobruska; one of them took the name Schœnfeld when he converted to Christianity. According to the report of the commissioners in charge of the Chabot affair, there were two Freys in Paris, three in Austria, and a sister maintained by a German baron. The report does not say whether it was this sister who became Madame Chabot. "These cunning and dangerous intriguers sneak up on people with great reputations and popularity, hoping by their false patriotism to earn their trust and reach the top positions in the Republic"[78].

One may wonder why the Freys, who enjoyed a very good fortune in Germany, since their lands were valued at two million, threw themselves into the revolutionary turmoil. The Court's bulletin answers: "The Freys, secret agents of foreign powers whose corruption they direct, etc.".

Emmanuel and Moïse Frey were in fact spies for the Austrian government, and provided enough service to earn them both the title of Baron[79]. The famous Baron de Trenck recounted that the elder Frey had come to Vienna to traffic in the beauty of his two very pretty sisters; they caused such a scandal that the Austrian government expelled them. Trenck knew this character perfectly well and knew that he was employed as a spy by the emperors

---

[77] Lenôtre: *Le Baron de Batz*, p. 45 ff. Baron de Batz: *La vie et les conspirations de J. de Batz.*

[78] Archives nationales, W. 342.648. L. Kahn: *Les Juifs à Paris pendant la Révolution.*

[79] Feuilles d'Histoire, 1er January 1914. Article by M. P. Bart.

Joseph and Leopold [80]. M. A. Mathiez believes him to be affiliated with Freemasonry and Weishaupt's Illuminati.

The Frey brothers, who were in regular contact with Ephraim, were probably also employed by the Prussian government.

Once in France, Moïse changed his name to Junius Frey. He and his brother joined the Jacobin club in Strasbourg, then the one in Paris (June 1791), and set up home at 19, rue d'Anjou. The two brothers gave excellent dinners, with regulars including Chabot, Lebrun Tondu, Fabre d'Églantine, Éphraïm, Ronsin, Prohly, Pereyra and Desfieux.

As members of the insurrection committee, the Freys paid considerable sums to maintain the cosmopolitan bands that fought on 20 June and 10 August[81]. They took part in the latter insurrection and were slightly wounded. This claim to fame did not prevent them from being arrested later. After the fall of the monarchy, the Freys seemed to switch to the service of the counter-revolutionaries and became agents of Jean de Batz[82].

It was at their instigation that Chabot and his friends shot the Girondins; but soon the Freys were arrested in their turn, along with Chabot, to whom they had arranged to marry their sister. They were accused of "spending two to three thousand francs a month on their table, while the people crushed themselves at the baker's door to get a piece of bread[83]". What was more serious, and what people did not dare to talk about too loudly, was the distribution of bribes at the Convention. One day for example, with the complicity of Delaunay and Julien (of Toulouse), Frey

---

[80] Recueil de Tuetey. Vol. X¹, p. 235.

[81] Sybel: *History of Europe*, I, p. 397.

[82] Archives nationales, F. 7 4774. 67.

[83] Archives nationales, F. 7 4637.

entrusted 150.000 livres to Chabot to cause a financial panic. Another day, as Fabre d'Églantine was violently attacking the Compagnie des Indes, Chabot was asked to give him 100,000 livres to silence him. He keeps the money and claims to have given it to Fabre[84].

In the interrogation of Diederichsen, the Frey brothers' factotum, the following question was asked: "Did Junius Frey not have frequent conferences with the Austrian emperor? Diederichsen replied: "I was aware of these conferences without knowing what they were about".

Junius and Emmanuel Frey were guillotined at the same time as Chabot.

Among the regulars at the Frey brothers' dinners, we have mentioned three names that appear frequently in the history of the Revolution:. Pereyra, Proly, Desfieux. Count Proly was the natural son of the Austrian minister Kaunitz; Pereyra (Juda de Jacob), a Portuguese Jew, was a tobacco merchant in the rue Saint-Honoré[85]; Desfieux was a Bordeaux wine merchant. By what chance do we always find them dining together at Madame de Ste Amaranthe's, speculating on the stock market in Red Sea shares, members of the Paris Commune's insurrection committee, and delegates from the Jacobin club to Dumouriez's army[86]. Pereyra, member of the club of St-Roch and assessor of the justice of peace of the district, is connected with Cloots, Hébert, Hérault de Séchelles and Ronsin; he takes part in all the riots, makes remove Kellermann from the club of the Jacobins, and asks for pursuits against him. He took part in the fall of the Girondins, worked to establish a triumvirate of Robespierre, Danton and Marat, and then, after the death of Louis XVI, joined

---

[84] Hamel: *Histoire de Robespierre*, t. III, p. 303.

[85] He started out as a jeweller in Bordeaux.

[86] Archives nationales. T. 1684.

the counter-revolutionaries. Pereyra, Proly and Desfieux head the list of de Batz secret agents[87].

Pereyra then had two residences, 55 and 105 rue St-Denis; denounced by Barbaroux, then by Robespierre, as being part of a foreign committee, Pereyra was arrested during the Terror and guillotined. The attestation report states that after "pruning a large number of useless papers, we squeezed the remainder into a basket that we sealed"[88]. This is followed by an enumeration of 96 letters in English, 92 documents in English, 73 documents in English, 68 documents in English, and so on. It is regrettable that these papers have disappeared; they would undoubtedly contain evidence of the action of the English government on Pereyra and his friends.

Alongside these well-known figures, a large number of Israelites played a modest role in the Revolution. Isaïe Spire was in charge of supplying the troops. Cerf Beer, a banker in the Faubourg Montmartre, was a supplier to the armies and a juror at the criminal court. The German Isaac Calmer, millionaire in clogs, president of the revolutionary club of Clichy, is known for his violence, while his brother Benjamin Calmer, stockbroker, remains a royalist; in this way the family has support in all parties. Despite suspicions about his patriotism, Benjamin Calmer was appointed commissioner for the liquidation of Philippe Égalité's assets. It is probably he who is described in the acts of the Commune as "Calmer seigneur de la terre d'Ailly". Isaac Calmer forgot to scrape the fleurs-de-lis from the chimneys of his château in Clichy-la-Garenne and was denounced by the families of several of his victims; the two brothers were guillotined at the end of the Terror[89].

---

[87] Archives nationales. F. 7 4774.

[88] Archives nationales. T. 1658.

[89] L. Kahn: *Jews in Paris.*

The German Heymen was a justice of the peace assessor in Paris. Isaïe Beer Bing, author of a volume on the Jews, is very close to Éphraïm and frequents revolutionary circles with him. He was a friend of Lafayette, Grégoire, Rœderer and Emmery.

Hazan is a member of the general surveillance committee. D'Acosta commanded a company of the national guard. Rosenthal commands the legion responsible for guarding the Temple. Calman is commissioner of the Petits Pères district. The Genévois Kermer is a member of the Tuileries club. The Dane Diederichsen was the Freys' most trusted man. The bankers Boyd and Kerr are Pitt's secret agents in Paris[90]. Z. Hourwitz, born in Lithuania, was a pedlar in Berlin and Paris, then curator of manuscripts in the King's library at the start of the Revolution. Under the Empire, he was a professor of foreign languages. Mayer, more occupied with speculation than politics, is said to have spent 300,000 livres on a single dinner offered after 9 Thermidor to ten ministers and deputies[91].

The revolutionary committee included Jacob Reis, Léon Azur, Fould, Weisweiler and others.

The Israelites of Paris formed an association whose leaders signed an address to the Constituent Assembly[92]. This document tells us that the president was Godschmit (perhaps Goldschmidt was meant), the vice-president Lagouna; Weil and Benjamin Fernandez were called electors; Lévi, Jacob, Pereyra, Trenelle, Elie, Weil, Delcampo and Brandon deputies.

Another petition signed by Mardochée (deputy) and Silveyra (agent) exposed the injustice suffered by the Jews of Paris: they were treated less well, it seemed, than their foreign co-

---

[90] Archives nationales. W 389 no. 904.

[91] Schmidt: *Table of the French Revolution.*

[92] Acts of the Paris Commune published by S. Lacroix, v. VII, p. 554.

religionists. And yet they were all "of the same family, descendants of Jacob son of Isaac"[93].

Here, moreover, is how the revolutionaries understood fraternity with regard to the Israelites, their allies: The decree of 16 Messidor, Year II, forbade Jews to follow the army on pain of death[94]. The newspaper *Le Propagateur*[95] complained that since the Revolution, the Frenchman was "exposed every day to dealing with a Jew, without any way of knowing that he is not dealing with a man, but with an enemy".

A mysterious figure called Falc played a certain role in secret societies at the end of the 18th[e] century. He is sometimes referred to as the Chief Rabbi. In his correspondence, Savalette de Langes simply calls him Doctor Falc. Of German origin, he lived mainly in London. He predicted that Philippe Égalité would take the throne[96].

In short, a very small group of Israelites quickly made a name for themselves and played an important role in the Revolution; but the Jews of France went unnoticed. The leaders of their co-religionists had arrived from abroad at the end of the reign of Louis XVI.

Contrary to what one might suppose, stock market speculation during the revolutionary period was mainly the preserve of Protestants.

The Jews mainly seized the furniture of castles and the treasures of churches, and became masters of landed property by

---

[93] Actes de la Commune de Paris, 2e série, t. IV, Mai 1791.

[94] The decree was signed by Laurent, the people's representative for the northern army.

[95] 17 Brumaire year VIII.

[96] P. Moniquet: *France in peril.*

means of usurious loans[97].

---

[97] Capefigue: *History of major financial transactions*. E. Drumont: *La France Juive*, t. I, p. 305.

CHAPTER IV

THE PROTESTANTS

The Judeo-Masonic coalition found such considerable support among the Protestants that M. Sourdat wrote a volume to establish that "the real authors of the Revolution are the Protestants" [98]. This is an obvious exaggeration, but the Protestants gave the Freemasons continual support. "One of the main founders of modern Freemasonry was J. Th. Désaguliers, the son of a Protestant pastor who was forced to leave France by the revocation of the Edict of Nantes" [99]. Settled in London, a friend and collaborator of Newton, J. Th. Désaguliers became, at the age of thirty-six, the third Grand Master of the Grand Lodge of England (1719).

Since Freemasonry was secretly attacking Catholicism, it must have had the sympathies of Protestants. Protestants, on the other hand, had not generally had much to commend them for under the French monarchy, and so at different times they were to be found in all the conspiracies. The result was a redoubling of rigorous measures, which led to political prosecutions being attributed to Catholic intolerance.

Long after Coligny's machinations with England against the

[98] Sourdat: *The true authors of La Révolution.*

[99] Minutes of *the sessions of the* 1889 *International Masonic Congress*, p. 36 (report by F Amiable).

King of France[100], the Duke of Bavaria organised in Germany, "at the request of the French Protestants, a real Huguenot crusade"[101] and prepared the invasion of our country in 1587. Under Louis XIII, Guiton, the Protestant mayor of La Rochelle, asked the English for help against the king[102]. Later, the Huguenots entered into intrigues with the Spanish. There are therefore extenuating circumstances for the persecutions directed against them by our monarchy.

Franklin pointed out that the English were working in the Cévennes to create, with the complicity of the Protestants, an independent province under British protectorate.

The unrest in Nîmes in 1790 was caused by Protestants massacring the Capuchins.

After the deplorable revocation of the Edict of Nantes, the eyes of French Protestants turned to England and Switzerland: in Geneva at the end of the 18th century there was a group of intelligent and active men whose influence was felt throughout Europe. These Protestants were also the world's leading financiers. This explains Necker's appointment to the Ministry of Finance.

It's not easy to form an opinion about this character, about whom much has been said both good and bad.

According to Ginguené[103] (member of the Institut), Necker "born a republican hated kings... born a Protestant, his secret vow was always to lose the clergy and discredit the Catholic

---

[100] See E. Renauld: *Le péril protestant*, p. 33 ff.

[101] Baguenault de Puchesse: *The failure of the German invasion in* 1587. (Correspondent of 25 November 1914.)

[102] Charles MAURRAS: *Religious politics.*

[103] Guinguené. *Necker,* 1796.

religion". His compatriot Clavière wrote to Isaac Cornuaud: "Necker has much more surface area than depth. I deny him the heart of an upright man and friend of humanity"[104].

But Clavière was open to question. When Napoleon Ier received Baron A. de Staël, Necker's grandson, he told him: "Your grandfather overthrew the monarchy; he led the king to the scaffold. Your grandfather overthrew the monarchy; he led the king to the scaffold"[105].

On the other hand, Necker found talented apologists, not only in his family, but among writers belonging to the most diverse opinions. He introduced some very useful reforms, including that of hospitals.

According to the Marquis de Ségur [106], "from the day Louis XVI accepted the ingenious remedy invented by Necker (the Estates General), the Revolution was only a matter of time". But in preparing for the Revolution, he was no doubt not thinking of sending Louis XVI and Marie-Antoinette to the scaffold. Like many constitutionalists, he did not believe that the conquest of liberty and the abolition of abuses should result in massacres and the revolutionary court.

Necker," says Ch. Dupuy, "was a muddler but not a revolutionary. His protégés from Geneva were less scrupulous and more daring[107].

Vergennes, who also called him a restless draft dodger, explained to the king the apprehension of the clergy at seeing his

---

[104] Memoirs of Isaac Cornuaud, recently published by Mlle Cherbuliez.

[105] Works by Baron de STAËL.

[106] *Le couchant de la monarchie*. T. II, p. 377.

[107] Louis XVI and the Genoese conspiracy. *Le Soleil*, 10 -August 1918.

natural enemy at the head of finance. He points out "the praise given to him in part of the British Parliament, whose factions all unite when it is necessary to hate and harm us[108].

Like all the Swiss, Necker was subject to English influence; he had almost married his daughter (Mme de Staël) to William Pitt. Burke told the House of Commons: "Mr Necker is our best friend on the continent". Moreover, the Necker family, who had settled in Geneva at the beginning of the eighteenth[e] century, were of Irish origin and had retained many ties with England.

A serious accusation against Necker can be found in Garran de Coulon's report to the Research Committee on the famine of 1789: Necker is said to have written to Bertier to have the rye cut before the harvest, so as to exacerbate the famine. Bertier did not carry out the order and was nevertheless massacred as a grabber[109].

We do not know what evidence Garran de Coulon relied on. Mirabeau wrote to Mauvillon at[110]: "Necker is well aware that his reign will be over the day order is re-established"; he said of Necker to Brunswick: "This mediocre financier would lose ten empires rather than compromise his self-esteem". But Mirabeau was the minister's enemy.

What seems to be better established is the participation of Necker's family in the troubles of 1789: his son-in-law, Baron de Staël Holstein, under the pretext of obtaining information, frequented the most exalted circles and informed the conspirators

---

[108] Marquis de Ségur : *Le couchant de la monarchie,* II, p. 413.

[109] *Report by Garran de Coulon,* p. 48. Bord. *The storming of the Bastille,* p. 33.

[110] *Mémoires de Mirabeau,* t. VIII, p. 20.

of what was happening in the King's Council[111].

When the revolutionary party had triumphed, M. de Staël held frequent negotiations with the Committee of Public Safety on behalf of the Protestant courts. On 6 December 1793, Soulavie handed Robespierre the conditions of the Protestant states of the north for recognition by the revolutionary government. One of the main conditions was the substitution of Protestantism for Catholicism in France. According to Ch. Dupuy, Robespierre agreed in principle. The question remained unresolved for a long time; later the Concordat, thwarting the hopes of the Protestants, was the real cause of Mme de Staël's animosity against Napoleon I[er112].

If we are to believe Léouzon Le Duc[113], Baron de Staël Holstein was a constitutionalist; it was his wife who pushed him towards the Jacobin party; in any case, he opposed the plans of the King of Sweden against the Revolution. In 1789, he felt that "the French nation lacks the qualities necessary for a free people". One might conclude from this that Staël was not working in favour of freedom, but in favour of the international conspiracy against France. As for Mme de Staël, Jacquet de la Douay, the king's prosecutor in the principality of Dombes, accused her of betraying the queen[114] and reported the astonishment felt by the ladies of the court who sent Mme de Staël into the good graces of Marie-Antoinette.

On the other hand, it is said that she later plotted with Narbonne to save the king and queen by buying land near Dieppe

---

[111] G. Bord: *La conspiration révolutionnaire de 1789*, p. 37.

[112] Ch. Dupuy, *Louis XVI et la conjuration Gènevoise.*

[113] *Preface to the diplomatic correspondence of Baron de Staël Holstein.*

[114] F. Descotes. *The French Revolution, as seen from abroad.*

and taking the royal family there in disguise[115].

Louis Necker, the minister's brother, belonged to the Amis Réunis lodge, whose revolutionary and international role we have explained. Lastly, his brother-in-law, Germain, was a member of the Propaganda Club, which organised the massacre of the bodyguards[116]: The Count of Vaudreuil repeated a remark made by Marie-Antoinette after the storming of the Bastille: "You were right," she told him, "Necker is a traitor; we are lost[117]. The Queen's opinion does not seem to be generally shared, but Necker was probably an unconscious instrument of the revolutionary plot. He enjoyed immense popularity for as long as he was deemed useful to the projects of the international syndicate, but fifteen months after his triumphant return, he resigned without anyone thinking of retaining him[118].

While it is true that Fersen shared Gustav III's opinion of Necker's guilt[119], Baron de Frénilly asserts, on the contrary, that this minister tried to stop the torrent whose dam he had opened[120].

On the other hand, Gustave Bord asserts that Freemasonry had given Necker the mission of preparing the Revolution. But, like most Freemasons, he was probably unaware of the sect's plans and may have had excellent intentions.

Finally, here is Mallet du Pan's assessment of Necker: "He seems to me to be one of the men who have done the most harm to this monarchy and justice only obliges me not to suspect his

---

[115] E. Welwert. *Around a lady-in-waiting.*

[116] Dasté. *Marie-Antoinette and the Terror.*

[117] Correspondence between Vaudreuil and the Count of Artois. Introduction.

[118] Bardoux. *Pauline de Beaumont*, p. 148.

[119] Lady Blennerhasset. *Mme de Staël et son temps*, t. II, p. 26 and 28.

[120] *Souvenirs of Baron de Frénilly*, p. 129.

intentions, but to pay tribute to his merit as administrator of finance...

By flattering popular ideas, M. Necker exaggerated them all... For a miserable reason of economy, he opposed the idea of holding the Estates General at a distance and fixed them at Versailles...[121]"

Two months later, Mallet du Pan wrote again to Mounier: "I have had positive information on Necker's account which leaves me in no doubt that he wanted the Revolution to take place to almost the full extent that it has been given[122].

But these lines, sent at the end of 1790, would certainly not have been written after the events of 1793; it is important to point this out. —

The edict of 28 November 1789 restored to Protestants the right to have their civil status (births, marriages and deaths) recorded, without being obliged to disguise their beliefs; a decree of 24 December 1789 restored to them all their civil rights and declared them eligible for all offices. They therefore no longer had any serious grounds for fighting the monarchy; but they were no doubt quite happy to take revenge on the Catholics for the long vexations they had suffered.

Mirabeau's slogan, "France must be decatholicised", did not just come from the Masonic lodges, but in all probability from the Protestants of Genoa, and the religious question was undoubtedly the real reason for the war in the Vendée and Brittany. The population of the West would have accepted the Republic perfectly well had it not been for the persecution of

---

[121] *Letter to Mounier.* 14th October 1790.

[122] 4th December 1790.

their priests.

It was also the civil constitution of the clergy that put Louis XVI at odds with the revolutionaries; this liberal sovereign, animated by good intentions, consented to all the reforms demanded by public opinion, but he was deeply religious; from the day the reformers wanted to proscribe the priests who had broken the oath, Louis XVI turned to the counter-revolutionaries. This anti-clerical movement was supported by the Protestants.

Mirabeau was largely responsible for confiscating the property of the clergy; he was obeying the instructions of his Gènevois committee.

At the same time, the English press was waging an anti-Catholic campaign. Barthélemy sent articles from London setting out the difficulty of establishing liberty in France without replacing papism with Protestantism[123]. "The Protestant party, it was added, had many supporters in the National Assembly[124].

In 1790, the number of temples and steps rapidly increased thanks to funds received from Geneva and Holland[125]. The Protestants' alliance with Freemasonry enabled them to continue worshipping during the Terror, while Catholic priests were imprisoned and guillotined[126].

A pastor, Rabaul St-Etienne, who had studied in Geneva and Lausanne, was appointed President of the National Assembly in March 1790. He told Mrs Stuart: "In less than two years our

---

[123] According to M. Bonald, "the political laws of England are sought only to come to the Anglican religion" (*Considérations sur la Révolution*, p. 74).

[124] Foreign Affairs Archives. London, c. 570.

[125] Durand. *History of Protestantism.*

[126] Aulard: *Studies and lessons on the Revolution.*

religion will generally dominate". Rabaul was the main cause of the troubles in Nîmes.

Several of his co-religionists also played an important role in the Revolution: Boissy d'Anglas, Jay, Cavaignac, Billaud-Varennes, Alquier, Julien (from Toulouse), Collot d'Herbais, Bernard, Lombard Lachaux, Jean Bon St-André, Dentzel, Grimmer, etc. Ten pastors were members of the Convention[127].

The role played by the Protestant Barnave is well known.

Moyse Bayle, whose first name suggests a Semitic origin, belonged to the Protestant religion; born in Geneva, he was deputy for Marseille, president of the Convention and member of the Committee of General Safety from September 1793 to September 1794. Arrested the following year, Moyse Bayle was amnestied and joined the police force.

Foreign Protestants played an even more important role in the Revolution than their French co-religionists.

The Protestants of Genoa, being at the head of finance, were bound to benefit, like the Israelites, from the stock market movements caused by the Revolution.

It is generally believed that speculation on the stock market is a recent phenomenon. What is recent is the prodigious increase in the number of securities; under Louis XVI, there was speculation in only four or five securities, Paris water, insurance, Red Sea shares, etc., but the differences between them were significant enough to make trading interesting. During the Revolution, there was also a lot of speculation on land and all commodities. Bidermann was particularly successful in

---

[127] Ernest Renauld. *The Protestant Peril.* Aulard. *Histoire politique de la Révolution,* p. 321.

speculating on grain. What profits were not made on foreign exchange! A thousand francs in gold were worth twenty-five thousand francs in scrip at certain times, then a few days later represented only five thousand. Lefebvre d'Acy wrote on 7 February 1792: "silver is at 55%"; on the following 10 March "silver is at 80%[128].

One day the louis was worth 200 livres at 11 o'clock, 250 at midday, then 500[129]. On 14 October 1795, it rose to 1255 livres.

Shares in the Compagnie des Indes fell by half in forty-eight hours. Shares in Les pompes à feu rose from 1,200 francs to 4,200 francs in the same week[130].

These fluctuations sometimes had unforeseen results: thus on 9 January 1793, the fall having been too strong, a hail of cane blows fell on the backs of the stockbrokers. Chabot's confession at his trial shows that the occult power behind the events sometimes offered large sums of money to certain members of the Convention to make proposals likely to cause a financial panic. The foreign syndicate which had announced in advance the storming of the Bastille, the condemnation of Louis XVI, etc., was thus able to make a magnificent difference by playing the downside for sure. As a result, great fortunes were made on the ruins of France. As a result, the *Nouvelles politiques* wondered (on 26 February 1795): "Was the Revolution nothing but bankers' speculation?

At the head of high finance were the Gènevois.

---

[128] P. de Vaissière. *Letter from aristocrats.*

[129] Louis Blanc. *History of the Revolution*, XII p. 116.

[130] D'Escherny. *Tableau historique de la Révolution.*

CHAPTER V

THE SWISS

At first glance, the events that unfolded between 1789 and 1794 in France seem to have been directed by the Swiss. In fact, Rousseau was often called the father of the Revolution; Necker prepared it; in 1793, Genevans occupied the Ministry of Finance, the Ministry of War, the Paris City Hall and a host of other posts; the Terror was organised by the Swiss Marat.

It is true that a great French figure dominated the early days of the Revolution, Mirabeau, but he was the instrument of a Geneva syndicate that made his speeches. This syndicate was made up of Etienne Dumont, Duroveray, Clavière and the pastor Salomon Reybaz[131], who were sometimes joined by the financier Panchaud.

Rivarol compared Mirabeau's head to a big sponge swollen with other people's ideas. However, it would be absurd to claim that Mirabeau did not have enough ideas of his own, and was not capable of making his own speeches; if, therefore, he was held in trusteeship by the Gènevois, there was an unknown cause for this: perhaps Mirabeau was bound by commitments made in the Masonic lodges and received the word of command from Geneva

---

[131] See the Fonds Reybaz (Manuscripts) at the Bibliothèque de Genève. It contains 59 letters from Mirabeau to Reybaz.

while other people took it from London. Perhaps it was a prosaic financial matter: Mirabeau frequently borrowed from the Swiss bankers Jeanneret and Schweitzer; as he was always short of money, the people of Genoa still held him by this means. When Mirabeau dealt with the court, he partially repaid Schweitzer, who was very surprised[132].

By a singular contradiction, the French monarchy seems to have been overthrown by the Swiss, while the king's most loyal defenders, the Swiss, are being slaughtered in his defence.

But the Geneva union represented a turbulent minority to which Necker, Mallet du Pan and the moderate minds in their country were totally hostile. We remember the revolutionary movement that broke out in Geneva in 1782. The minister Vergennes, whose high intelligence has not always been sufficiently admired, wrote at the time: "I am studying the quarrels of the revolutionaries of Geneva, because it is to be feared that their writings will carry outside the fanaticism with which they are filled." As Mallet du Pan observed, it was indeed the French Revolution that was brewing in Geneva in 1782[133].

After the troubles of this period, a Helvetic club was founded in Paris by Castella; Doctor Kolly was its secretary. Here is how this club was assessed by a Swiss official, Muller[134]: "This infamous society was made up of galley slaves, bandits and other scoundrels from a nation whose name was being disgraced... The cantons resolved to request the surrender of these malefactors, but our dear allies, instead of corresponding with us according to the treaties, continued to protect this unworthy troupe." Castella had in fact been condemned in Switzerland to be drawn and

---

[132] A. Stern. *Life of Mirabeau.*

[133] *Memoirs of Mallet du Pan,* ch. 1 and 3. Sorel. *Europe and the French Revolution,* p. 141 and 142.

[134] *Letter from Barthélémy.* Foreign Affairs Archives. Switzerland, v. 428.

quartered. Marat, Duport and Menou joined the Swiss club. Sillery and Barnave promised him their protection. This club, which made frequent appeals to Schweitzer's purse, was successively known as the Club Helvétique and the Société Helvétique; it had its headquarters in rue du Regard, rue Ste-Marguerite, rue du Sépulcre and in a room in the abbey of St-Germain de Prés, granted by the district of that name.

In 1792, the Club Helvétique became the Club des patriotes étrangers, also known as the Club des nations étrangères amies de la Constitution. On 10 August it changed its name again to the Club des Allobroges[135]; one of its most active members was Doctor Doppet, who introduced a number of Savoyards into the association, including Doctor Dessaix, the notary Frezier, the public prosecutor Souviran, the poet Michel Chastel, the lawyer Turinaz, the surgeon Magnin, Ganem and Bussat.

Members of the Club Helvétique were constantly distributing seditious pamphlets to soldiers. A decree was issued on 19 September 1790 to put a stop to their activities, but they appear to have continued in secret.

Mirabeau's inspirers belonged to a more enlightened and cultivated milieu. So what was this union all about? The Duroveray file in the National Archives[136] provides the answer: Duroveray, Clavière, Étienne Dumont and Divernois were exiled from Geneva in 1782 when the French and Swiss armies restored order there. Clavière settled in France; Duroveray, Divernois and Dumont went to London, taking with them the desire to take as much revenge on the French nation as they could. In London they made contact with all the people who were most likely to help them in their plans for revenge.

---

[135] Mathiez. *La Révolution et les étrangers,* p. 33 ff.

[136] F. 7, 6468.

Duroveray, public prosecutor in Geneva, had been dismissed at Vergenne's request. Thirty-five years old," says the police description, "he doesn't look it. He is an active and intelligent man. At the end of the reign of Louis XVI, he became a naturalised Irishman. He attended the sessions of the Estates General; some deputies protested against the presence of "a pensioner of the English government who takes part in the deliberations and sends notes and observations to the deputies[137]"—In fact, Duroveray received a pension of three hundred louis from the English ministry. —Mirabeau declares that this man is a martyr of liberty, Duroveray, to whom M. de Vergennes has made lose his position in Geneva. "Great applause. Duroveray is surrounded by deputies who come to him.

After 10 August, Duroveray was offered the Ministry of Justice, which he refused, and then he was attached to the French embassy in London. Bonnecarrère, the chargé d'affaires, pointed out that it was dangerous to entrust the secrets of our diplomacy to a foreigner. Lebrun Tondu answers: "Duroveray was attached in spite of me to the embassy of London, by the protection of Brissot, Clavière and Roland, although he was well recognized pensionnaire of England".

He added that Duroveray's assignment would be withdrawn next month[138].

Complaints having accumulated against Duroveray, Lebrun decided to recall him on 19 October. Back in Paris, Duroveray was eventually denounced as an agent of the English government. A police report states that on 4 May 1793, at half past midnight, Duroveray was asked to disclose his correspondence with England. This citizen," say the officers in charge of his arrest, "presented us with several packets, which he

---

[137] *Foreign Office archives,* London. v. 582.

[138] *Foreign Office archives,* London. v. 582.

told us contained the said correspondence, which appears to be from 1789 to the present. The seals were affixed. On July 30, the Supervisory Committee considering that "in said papers there are shorthand and English (it was said), that the committee has no knowledge of these kinds of characters and languages, decides that the box, wallet and packages will be brought to the Committee of Public Safety[139]. ".

Then silence fell over the papers in question, which were no longer in the National Archives.

Etienne Dumont, a contemporary Gènevois pastor and friend of Duroveray, "has a lot of wit, speaks well and with reserve[140]". Highly esteemed in London by Fox, Lord Holland, etc., Dumont received a pension of three hundred louis from Lord Lansdowne[141].

Introduced to Mirabeau in 1788 by Sir Samuel Romilly, he settled in Paris the following year and inspired Mirabeau's speeches, sometimes taking advice from Lord Elgin[142]. In 1791, Dumont stayed at Bidermann's house, where Reybaz, Clavière and Brissot also frequented. He contributed to the newspaper *Le Républicain*. Barthélemy's papers show that Etienne Dumont and Duroveray were among Pitt's most active agents in Paris[143].

Divernois (or d'Ivernois), expelled from Geneva with Duroveray, Dumont and Clavière, was like them pensioned by England. "A few years younger than his friends, slim, walking

---

[139] *Archives nationales. F. 7., 4696.*

[140] *National Archives. F. 7., 6468.*

[141] Letter from Mme Reybaz to her brother (*The life and conspiracies of Jean de Batz, by Baron de Batz).*

[142] *Memoirs of Etienne Dumont.*

[143] *Letter from Jeanneret to Deforgues, 19 February, 1794.*

with his head forward, Divernois offered nothing distinguished in his overall physique; on the other hand, he was very amiable in society, very witty, spoke easily, wrote well, with energy and ease[144].

Secret correspondence from the Berlin court[145] lists Divernois as one of Pitt's main agents. On the other hand, he never approved of revolutionary cruelties, and saved the life of General de Montesquiou.

Convicted in absentia during the Terror, Divernois settled in England and became a naturalised Irishman. In 1814, he returned to Gènevois and was appointed Councillor of State.

Clavière was "inseparable from Dumont and Duroveray", say the reports to the Committee of Public Safety. Our chapter on the Israelites explains Clavière's political role.

Pastor Salomon Reybaz gave many of Mirabeau's speeches at the start of the Revolution. He received a pension from England[146]. During the Terror, he went unnoticed; under the Directoire, he was Switzerland's minister in France.

On 29 November 1796, Reybaz was asked to leave Paris within twenty-four hours. The only comment on this in the newspapers was that "this Gènevois arouses neither the curiosity nor the interest of the citizens[147].

So the whole Genoese group, whose role was so important in

---

[144] *Archives nationales,* f. 7, 6468.

[145] Karmin. *Documents relating to secret correspondence with the Berlin court.*

[146] *Soulavie's memoirs.* Reybaz's manuscripts in Geneva. *History* of *the counter-revolution* (baron de Batz).

[147] Aulard. *Paris under the Thermidorian reaction.* T. III, p. 598.

our Revolution, was simply an instrument of the English government.

Pache is a peculiar revolutionary: peaceful and patriarchal, the son of caretakers is the model for ministry employees. Every morning he arrived on foot from the suburbs with a small loaf of bread in his pocket and worked all day. Introduced by Necker to the control of finances, he made friends with the wealthy Anacharsis Cloots, Chabot, Hassenfralz and the most exalted Jacobins. He represented the Luxembourg section on 3 August 1792, for the petition calling for the deposition of the king. *Papa Pache,* as he was known, fraternised with the massacres of September[148]; he was given the Ministry of War by the protection of Roland, whose indispensable factotum he had become, and then he set about losing his benefactor and the Girondins. He displayed great intelligence and activity in disorganising the national defence and preparing the defeat of the French armies. In the end, as "all the generals, all the commissioners of the Convention, accused Pache at the same time[149]", he was stripped of his portfolio. La Réveillère Lépeaux called Pache the greatest squanderer of the public purse: in three months of ministry, he left one hundred and sixty million unaccounted for; Barère declared that in view of the impossibility of unravelling Pache's accounts, it would be better to pass the sponge[150].

Pache's dubious reputation did not prevent him from being appointed mayor of Paris; in this capacity, he signed the minutes that were to bring down Marie-Antoinette's head. He had Dillon guillotined and delivered the cannon to the Paris Commune during the Terror. Every evening he sent his wife, daughter and sister to the Federated barracks to incite them against the

---

[148] G. Lenôtre. *Veilles maisons, vieux papiers.* t. I, p. 264.

[149] Chuquet. *Dumouriez.*

[150] Sybel. *History of Europe*, vol. II, p. 113.

Girondins[151].

Cambon believes that at the time of the insurrection of May 31, Pache was bribed by the counter-revolutionaries: the movement would have been "prepared by Robespierre, Pache and Danton to restore the small Capet on the throne[152]" On the other hand, as Pache believed he could achieve dictatorship, he may have encouraged all the riots in the hope of profiting from them. In the spring of 1794, the Cordeliers were plotting to put Pache at the head of a new government. Hébert agreed.

Reports from the Ministry of the Interior referred to Pache as an agent of Pitt and added: "It is claimed that if he had not been imprisoned, he would have prevented the establishment of the new constitution (20 November 1795)[153].

Pursued several times, arrested at the same time as Hébert, Pache escaped the guillotine, no doubt thanks to the power of the international union. When the Revolution was over, Pache retired, having made his fortune, to an old abbey he had bought at a low price, which he had turned into a magnificent estate. He lived there quietly, no longer having any relations with his old friends, and no longer even reading the newspapers.

His son renounced his opinions and changed his name[154]. His son-in-law, Xavier Andouin, was a member of the Paris Commune and an ordnance officer; it was he who one day asked the Legislative Assembly, on behalf of the Jacobin Club, for a law to shorten proceedings in order to eliminate the defence of

---

[151] Sybel. *History of Europe*, vol. II, p. 32.

[152] A. Lanne. *The mystery of Quiberon.*

[153] Tureau Dangin, *Royalists and Republicans*. Aulard. *Paris sous la réaction Thermidorienne*, t. II, p. 411.

[154] Lenôtre. *Vieilles maisons, Vieux papiers*, t. I, p. 272.

the accused.

Pache seems to have been a conscientious and hard-working employee of the occult power that was directing events. This was also the opinion of Robespierre, who was never able to catch him in the act.

Marat has been attributed several nationalities, including French[155]. However, according to civil status records, Marat's father was from Cagliari in Sardinia, and became Swiss after marrying a woman from Genoa.

This friend of the people was born in Switzerland, practised medicine in Newcastle and London from 1769 to 1777, joined Freemasonry and then became physician to the guards of the Comte d'Artois; his violent attacks on Necker led to his prosecution in 1790. He returned to England, only to come back as soon as anarchy was established in Paris. The rest of his story is well known. With regard to Marat, let us simply note that most of the violence and cruelty of the revolutionary period was perpetrated by foreigners.

L'ami du peuple seems to have been an agent of Philippe Égalité; according to some authors, he was paid directly by England. It is said that Marat and Pitt met in London in a small tavern room (in 1792)[156].

Marat's place in history is astonishing: it cannot be seriously claimed that he was talented either as a writer or an orator. He was generally unsympathetic and, according to Taine, he suffered from a type of madness well known to psychiatrists, delusions of

---

[155] Mr R. Poidebard tells us of a Lyon tradition according to which the Marat family came from Chuyer in the Rhône. M. Chèvremont attributes a Spanish origin to him.

[156] See Despatys. *La Révolution, la Terreur, le Directoire*, p. 49.

ambition.

Hulin (or Hullin), of Swiss origin, was the manager of the laundry at La Briche, near St Denis; in 1789 he joined the French Guards and was among the victors at the Bastille. From then on, he declared himself to be a hero; a memorandum in which Hutin and Maillard recount their exploits to the Assembly contains this sentence: "If it is permissible to praise themselves, the undersigned will no doubt do so, but with the modesty that so well describes the character of true heroes"[157].

Hulin formed the company of Bastille volunteers and became its commander. Complaints soon arose against his management; Marat also accused him of leading bandits expelled from the Parisian battalions[158]; and a group of Bastille victors denounced him as a "police informer"[159].

After commanding the national guard during the October days, Hulin distinguished himself on 10 August. When the national guard was disbanded, he was appointed captain in the army of the North. Arrested under the Terror, he escaped the guillotine; he was again president of the council of war that condemned the Duc d'Enghien, and then became a general under the Empire. Hulin was pistol-whipped by the conspirator Malet, breaking his jaw, but he recovered. Under the Restoration, he offered his services to Louis XVIII, who refused.

A large number of Swiss played a minor role in the Revolution: Necker had been brought to power largely through the influence of Masson de Pezay, whose father was from Genoa. Pezay was the lover of the princesse de Montbarey, who led Mme de Maurepas; she led her husband, who led the king. Maurepas

---

[157] *Actes de la Commune de Paris*, t. I, p. 156.

[158] *Actes de la Commune de Paris*, t. I, p. 156.

[159] Buchez and Roux. *Parliamentary History*, t. VIII, p. 277.

therefore claimed that Pezay was the true king of France. The recall of the parliaments was due to his influence.

Christin, secretary at the Ministry of Finance, was more of a counter-revolutionary, while Finguerlin was a member of the Lyon Commune and the departmental directoire.

La Harpe, who called Voltaire "papa", was born in Paris of Swiss parents. He seduced the daughter of a lemon merchant, married her, divorced her and remarried at the age of fifty-eight to a twenty-three year old girl. In 1776, he became a member of the Académie Française.

Representative of the Commune for the district of St-Germain des Près, he never ceased to praise the Revolution in his lectures and works, wrote violent articles in the *Mercure de France,* and did not change his opinion either after the massacres or after the death of Louis XVI. But he was arrested in April 1794, and his fellow prisoners, the bishops of St-Brieuc and Montauban, converted him [160]. According to Mallet du Pan, an unknown woman had La Harpe read the Imitation of Jesus Christ during his captivity, and this was the real reason for his conversion [161]. Be that as it may, the former Voltairien who had become a cleric took the Revolution "with an aversion equal to the love he had borne it" [162].

The Directoire ordered his arrest for the second time in 1796; editor of the *Mémorial,* La Harpe was involved in royalist agitation, acquitted and then again sentenced to deportation [163]; he managed to go into hiding from 18 Fructidor to 18 Brumaire. The

---

[160] Ste-Beuve. *Lundis.* Tome V.

[161] Mallet du Pan, *Mémoires*, p. 459.

[162] Arnault. *Souvenir of a sixty-year-old.*

[163] *Recueil des actes du Directoire exécutif.* T. I.

police forgot about him and he died in 1803, leaving a number of famous works.

Another Gènevois, Pictet, a friend of Voltaire, settled in Paris about ten years before the Revolution, found a position thanks to Necker and frequented Mme Roland's salon; he was one of the founders of the Société des amis des noirs. But during the Terror he changed sides, and Barthélemy's papers mention Pictet and Mallet du Pan as being very active with the help of the English against the Convention.

Mallet du Pan always adopted a moderate and wise attitude, criticising revolutionary excesses and denouncing the existence of an occult power, without however mentioning the Masonic organisation. He wrote to the King of Prussia about the revolutionary clubs: "All these societies are, without suspecting it, dominated by the secret influence of a more intimate assembly composed of the quintessence of all the other assemblies:... This secret assembly is composed of a central committee residing in Paris, corresponding with other central committees...

Jacobinism is allied with the Presbyterians in England, the Illuminati in Germany, etc."[164].

Before the Revolution, Mallet du Pan wrote the *Journal historique et politique* de Genève, which was merged with the *Mercure de France;* in it he defended the ideas of the constitutional monarchists. Louis XVI entrusted him with a secret mission to the coalition forces. Returning to Geneva after the fall of the monarchy, he maintained an active correspondence in favour of the monarchists. He died in London in 1800, having written several valuable works.

In the opposite camp was Virchaud (de Neufchâtel) secretary

---

[164] F. Descostes. *The French Revolution as seen from abroad.*

of the Cordeliers club; it was he who submitted to the Assembly the petition of 15 July 1791 against royalty[165]. It was rumoured that the petitioners had been bribed by foreign governments.

Gaspard Schweitzer (from Zurich), nephew of Lavater, seems to have been a good man exploited by the international syndicate. Affiliated with the Illuminés, he settled in Paris at the start of the Revolution; introduced by Mirabeau to the Jacobins, he made friends with Barnave, Robespierre, Bergasse, etc., and allowed himself to be duped and ruined by the revolutionaries, who never ceased to make use of his purse. Mirabeau, while borrowing considerable sums from him, courted Mme Schweitzer, who is said to have spurned him.

In 1794, the Committee of Public Safety instructed Schweitzer to go to America to sell the main riches of the royal castles, and to claim thirty million lent by Louis XVI to the United States. Schweitzer was delighted and saw this as an opportunity to rebuild his fortune. Unfortunately, he was joined by an adventurer called Swan, who robbed him. He returned to Europe and ended his life in misery[166].

Niquille, an agent of the Paris Commune, became Inspector General of Police after 18 Brumaire. Arrested in spite of Barras following the explosion on 2 Nivôse, he was deported to Madagascar.

Panchaud, after having been a banker in London, was appointed director of the Caisse d'Escompte de Paris. Although he was part of the group leading Mirabeau, he seems to have been more concerned with finance than politics.

Gustave Bord attributed Foullon's death to influences from

---

[165] Aulard. *Histoire politique de la Révolution Française,* p. 148 ff.

[166] Barbey. *The Swiss outside Switzerland.*

Genoa and Sweden, without giving names.

Pastor Frossard (from Nyon) was an honorary director of the Oxford faculty and a member of the farmers' societies of Bath and Manchester. Young went to stay with him in Paris because he considered him almost a compatriot; linked with Brissot and Roland, Frossard was appointed after the flight from Varennes as a member of the Jacobin standing committee set up in Lyon, then as a member of the general council, and as public prosecutor. Accepted by the Jacobins of Clermont, he inaugurated Protestant worship in the Carmes church. He was in Lyon at the end of 1793 and then lost track of him until he was found in 1802 as a member of the Paris consistory[167].

Mr G. Bord[168] pointed out the strange attitude of Colonel d'Affry, who, after declaring himself ill at the time of the Réveillon affair, refused on 10 August to give the Swiss the order to fire on the rioters who were attacking them[169]. D'Affry belonged to the Freemasons.

In short, a group of Swiss played an important role in the Revolution, but they represented neither the policy of the Helvetic government nor the ideas of the majority of their country. Many of them were British pensioners; others were under British influence. In 1802, Napoleon Ier attributed the insurrection in Geneva to English influence.

Like the Freemasons, the Jews and the Protestants, the Swiss were an instrument of demolition directed by an occult power. In the opinion of Soulavie, the French resident in Geneva, "Dumont, Duroveray, Clavière and other adventurers were the henchmen

---

[167] *Correspondance de Mme Roland,* p. 726.

[168] *The revolutionary conspiracy of 1789.* G. Bord.

[169] See the *Moniteur* of 30 August 1792, p. 553.

of an English committee[170].

---

[170] *Soulavie memoir.* V. VI, p. 409.

CHAPTER VI

THE FOREIGN INVASION IN 1789

At the beginning of the Revolution, "Englishmen, Italians and bankers infiltrated the people's assemblies and the ministers' anterooms. They spied on everything and slipped into popular societies. Soon you see them linked to the magistrates who protect them"[171]. According to Loustalot and Thureau Dangin, there were 40,000 foreigners in Paris with no fixed address and no specific occupation[172]. Bezenval recounts that the appearance of these men, "most of them in disguise, armed with large sticks, was enough to make you realise what you had to fear from them". They would be the army employed by the revolutionary syndicate; they would be joined by the thousands of vagrants, thieves and down-and-outs who always rejoiced in times of unrest. "By careful selection, a corps of triple-paid janissaries would be formed"[173], who would carry out all the riots ordered by the occult power. The Duc d'Orléans' agents appear to have been responsible for paying this revolutionary army. According to the memoirs of Mallet du Pan[174], the pay was triple that of the regular troops.

---

[171] *Archives nationales* AD¹ 108. Report to the Convention on foreign factions.

[172] Thureau Dangin, *Royalists and Republicans*.

[173] TAINE. *The French Revolution.*

[174] *Mémoires de Mallet du Pan*, t. II, p. 52.

Marat acknowledged in *L'Ami du peuple*[175] that the victors of the Bastille were mostly Germans. The troop of General Henriot, a former servant who had been expelled several times for theft, consisted mainly of Germans who did not even understand French. M. de Montmorin stated that "almost all those who forced open the gates of the Tuileries on 21 June were foreigners"[176].

It should be noted in connection with this famous riot that two of the spectators, who were among the most intelligent, assign it the date of the 21st and not the 20th. The memoirs of General Dumouriez agree on this subject with the memorial of St Helena (L. 1, p. 106). This is one of the rare points on which these two mortal enemies (Napoleon and Dumouriez) are of the same opinion.

When, on the eve of 10 August, the ministers declared that the king would never agree to fire on his own people, Lameth replied: "Are the people to be found in a bunch of foreigners without a homeland who have been called into Paris for the last six months?"[177] .

The fact was so hard to deny that the directoire of the department of the Seine officially replied to a circular from the minister Roland: "We have not sought the opinion of the people in the midst of these gatherings of mostly foreign men"[178].

In his book on Frédéric Gentz, Schmidt Weissenfels also talks about the flood of adventurers that swept through France at this time, arriving from the banks of the Tiber as well as the banks of

---

[175] N° 50.

[176] G. MALET. *Winners of the Bastille and winners of* 10 August. *Intermédiaire des chercheurs* 10 February 1913.

[177] *Mémoires de Lameth*, p. 156.

[178] TAINE. *The Jacobin conquest.*

the Sprée.

It was not impossible to find French revolutionary officers to command these troops, but they did not seem to be sufficiently unscrupulous, and the conspirators chose a Pole, Lazowski, who had joined the French army and been sentenced to death for striking one of his superiors. Although pardoned by Louis XVI, he remained an enemy of royalty. An artillery captain at the start of the events of 1789, he was appointed a member of the Revolutionary Committee, Finistère section[179]. After organising the first disturbances, he was chosen on 16 June 1792, along with a few obscure citizens, to go to the Hôtel de Ville to announce the intention of the suburbs to rise up en masse. He then proposed to the Commune Council that the demonstrators should be armed "as a precaution and to impose their weapons on the ill-intentioned". Lazowski led the rioters on 20 June and 10 August, exposing himself to fire while the instigators of the movement went into hiding. He had the prisoners of Orleans put to death without trial with the help of Fournier the American, directed the massacres of Versailles, plotted with Desfieux and Varlet the assassination of the principal deputies of the right, and proposed to the Cordeliers the proscription of the Girondins.

He indulged in such excessive drinking that he died an alcoholic on 21 April 1793. Two months earlier he had been prosecuted for organising unrest in Amiens. However, the prison register for Amiens shows that Joseph-Félix Lazowski was locked up on 1er February 1794[180]. He had been dead for ten months. The explanation has yet to be found.

Perhaps it was his brother, tutor to the sons of the Duc de Liancourt, devoted to the royalist cause. Lacretelle said that Lazowski "moans about the sad fame attached by his brother to

---

[179] *Archives nationales*, F. 7, 2517.

[180] Darsy. *Amiens during the Revolution.*

his name[181]". In that case, there may be a first name error in the Amiens registers.

The great man was given a state funeral. The Jacobin club decided that Lazowski's bust should be placed next to that of Brutus, above the president's chair. Lazowski's reputation was rather mediocre; his funeral oration contains this sentence: "To the services rendered by Lazowski to the Revolution, it would be vain to level accusations of embezzlement, founded perhaps, and other offences all too familiar to men of great character".

But Robespierre declares that he weeps "over the immense loss that the Republic has just made and which absorbs all the faculties of its soul[182]."

In Alsace, the main agent of the revolutionary plot was a defrocked German monk, Euloge Schneider. A professor in Bonn in 1789, he moved to Strasbourg for no known reason and became known for his violence at the Jacobin Club. Immediately appointed judge and then accuser at the Revolutionary Court, he organised the Terror, levied huge fines on the whole city, put two thousand people in prison and had them treated more or less harshly depending on how much they paid him[183]. He travelled the length and breadth of Alsace, dragging his court and his guillotine in his wake, abusing women by terrorising them.

As long as he was content to rob, rape and guillotine, the Convention commissioners let him get away with it, but did he not one day have the idea of entering Strasbourg in a coach harnessed to six horses! This time, democratic equality was threatened; St-Just and Lebas issued the following decree: "The representatives of the people, informed més that Schneider came

---

[181] De Lacretelle. *Dix ans d'épreuves*, p. 67 ff.

[182] E. Biré. *Journal d'un bourgeois de Paris*, t. II p. 339 ff.

[183] Sybel. *History of Europe*, vol. II, p. 347.

to Strasbourg with insolent pomp, dragged by six horses, surrounded by guards with his sabre bare, decide that the said Schneider will be exposed tomorrow from 10 a.m. to 2 a.m. on the scaffold, to expiate the insult to the morals of the Republic and will then be taken to the Committee of Public Safety".

Schneider was sent to Paris, sentenced to death on 11 Germinal year II, and executed.

Desfieux (or Deffieux) is portrayed in Meillan's memoirs as a "rascal, thief, fraudulent bank robber, but a good patriot". Why was this good patriot, who was Belgian, so keen to overthrow Louis XVI instead of continuing the wine trade in Bordeaux that he had been running since 1789?

How did he get involved with Count Proly, Pereyra and Dubuisson? So many mysteries.

This is how he himself describes his beginnings in political life, without explaining his motives[184]:

"... On 12 July, I brought the news of Necker's dismissal to the Palais Royal and immediately urged people there to take up arms against the Court... On 13 July, I was one of the first to go to the church of the Petits Pères. There I gave the method of enrolment to form the national guard; this method was adopted.

On the 14th, I was at the Bastille and wherever else a patriot should be...

Business took me to Bordeaux. There I preached the Revolution and formed a popular society known as the Club du café national... I left at the invitation of the municipality of Toulouse to establish a popular society there... My reputation as

---

[184] *Archives nationales*, F. 7, 4672.

a patriot led me to be admitted to the Jacobin society... I was one of the first to denounce the Brissotins, the Rolandins, the Girondins...".

In August 1790, a peddler selling anti-militarist pamphlets was arrested; the investigation proved that he had been commissioned to do so by Desfieux, who had recently moved to Paris. The following year, Desfieux was appointed treasurer of the Jacobins, then a juror at the revolutionary court, chairman of the Jacobins club's committee of correspondence and a member of the revolutionary committee.

The Minister of War, Bouchotte, entrusted him with a mission in Switzerland. On his return to Paris, he supported the most advanced proposals and criticised the slowness of the revolutionary court.

In January 1793, Desfieux was vice-president of the Society of Friends of Liberty, which declared itself permanent until the execution of the tyrant and sent a delegation to invite the Commune to redouble its surveillance[185]. But at the same time, Desfieux was a secret agent of Baron de Balz, who wanted to try and save the king[186].

In the spring of 1793, Desfieux, a member of the insurrection committee, set up an office at his home in rue des Filles St-Thomas, where he traded places. He also took it upon himself to act on Collot d'Herbois in return for an honest brokerage. He was convinced that he had received money from Lebrun Tondu to intercept Jacobin dispatches, although it is not known for what purpose. Sometimes he simply made their correspondence disappear; sometimes he replaced it with false dispatches; the

---

[185] Beauchesne. *History of Louis XVII.*

[186] *Archives nationales*, F. 7, 4672.

couriers were paid handsomely to do this[187].

This enigmatic character was the owner of the house where Proly lived and one of his servants or employees was the keeper of the seals at the time of the arrest of Kaunitz's son[188]. Locked up almost at the same time as Proly, Desfieux managed to get out of prison on 25 Frimaire and demanded that the seals affixed to his house be lifted. It turned out that the seal had been broken by an unknown hand and the incriminating papers had disappeared.

In the end, Desfieux was sentenced to death along with his friends Pereyra and Proly.

One of her fellow citizens, the girl Terwagne, better known as Théroigne de Méricourt, was born in Belgium at the very moment, say the chroniclers of the time, "when Venus entered into conjunction with Mercury". This could have been seen as a dangerous omen. She went wrong at a very young age and became the mistress of an Austrian colonel and, it is said, of the King of England; false letters from Théroigne to this sovereign have been published. After various adventures that ended with her being sentenced to prison in Autrice, Théroigne de Méricourt settled in Paris shortly before the Revolution. She was often seen alone in a box at the Opéra, covered in diamonds[189]. Together with Romme, she founded the Club des *Amis de la Loi (Friends of the Law* Club), of which she was archivist, and thus found herself in frequent contact with Roland, Bosc and Lanthenas. She was admitted to the Cordeliers club in February 1790, where she gave a much-applauded speech.

At the meeting of 26 January 1792, Dufourny spoke in these terms at the Jacobins Club: "Gentlemen, I must announce to you

---

[187] Buchez and Roux. *Parliamentary History*, T. XXXI, p. 376.

[188] *Archives nationales.* F. 7, 2774.

[189] *Memoirs of the Comte d'Espinchal.*

a triumph for patriotism: Mademoiselle Théroigne, famous for her civic-mindedness and the persecutions she has suffered at the hands of tyranny, is here in the ladies' gallery. Immediately, several members of society brought her up and brought her down to the hall, where she was received with all the interest that her sex and her misfortunes could arouse[190].

However, as it is difficult to please everyone, a few days later Théroigne was publicly whipped by a group of counter-revolutionary women who met her at the Tuilerie. Collot d'Herbois did not like her either; on 23 April 1792 he declared in the gallery of the Jacobin Club: "What gives us great satisfaction is to learn that in a café, on the terrace of the Feuillants, Mademoiselle Théroigne has decided to withdraw her esteem from Robespierre and myself. At that moment, says the parliamentary history[191], Mademoiselle Théroigne was in the ladies' gallery. Irritated by the apostrophe and the rumour it created, she leapt over the barrier that separated her from the interior of the room, overcoming the efforts made to restrain her, she approached the desk with animated gestures, and insisted on asking to speak. But at last she was turned away from the room.

Théroigne de Méricourt featured in all the riots; she harangued the Parisians and the Flanders regiment on 5 and 6 October, after having preached revolt to the Nancy garrison. A pretty twenty-year-old brunette, according to the memoirs of Hyde de Neuville, dressed like an Amazon with a feathered Henri IV hat, a pair of pistols and a dagger in her belt, she incited the people to the massacre of the Swiss on 10 August and had the journalist Suleau, whose articles attacked her, slit his throat; she then had the unfortunate writer's head carried around on the end of a pike.

---

[190] Aulard: *La société des Jacobins*, t. III, p. 346.

[191] Buchez et Roux, t. XIV, p. 130.

General Thiébault recounts in his memoirs how his cannons were taken from him by Théroigne. After 10 August, it was Théroigne who overcame the resistance of the president of the Feuillants section to hand over the prisoners. Of course, they were immediately massacred.

Such exploits deserved to be rewarded, so the federates awarded civic crowns to Théroigne de Méricourt and Rose Lacombe, in memory of their courage on 10 August[192].

Why was this foreigner so passionate about the revolutionary cause? Where did the money she distributed to the rioters come from? One wonders whether she was simply the agent of the King of England or of Kaunitz, with whom she kept up a regular correspondence. The Vienna archives bear witness to this. It was not possible to collect her confidences afterwards, as she went mad in 1794 and was interned at the Salpêtrière hospital[193].

Among the Desfieux, Proly and Pereyra gang was the Spaniard Gusman (or Guzman). A shady banker, he tried unsuccessfully to pass himself off as the son of the Elector of Cologne, then as Grand of Spain, then as a descendant of the Dukes of Brittany. Under Louis XVI, he called himself Baron de Frey, a German subject, then joined the French army, from which he was expelled for unknown reasons. He became one of the most active agents of the Central Revolutionary Committee and the Revolutionary Committee of the Commune. The Piques section made him one of its commissioners. He was involved in all the troubles, spending money without counting the cost; Barbaroux and others reported him as distributing assignats to the rioters. M. Morel Fatio[194] believes that Guzman was an agent of

---

[192] *Mémoires de Bertrand de Molleville... Mémoires de Beaulieu.* Lacour : *Three women of the Revolution.*

[193] *Archives nationales,* F. 7, 4775, 27.

[194] *Historical Review.*

the Austrian government. Among the many denunciations against Guzman is one in which he is accused of being a woman disguised as a man.

Three times a week Gusman gave dinners at which Danton, Fabre d'Églantine, Camille Desmoulins, Pereyra, Chabot and a few Englishmen tasted wines supplied by Desfieux. He was a member of the Hébertistes, and after the death of Louis XVI, Gusman was one of Jean de Batz's secret agents[195].

He was condemned and guillotined on 5 April 1794.

The Italian Rotondo had been expelled from France in 1785 for swindling some twenty dancers at the Opéra. He is thought to have been enlisted by Lameth for the first riots of the Revolution. Together with his fellow citizen Cavallanti, he led the looting of the Hôtel de Castries. A few days later, he was beaten up by officers who didn't like his revolutionary tirades. He claimed to be a professor of foreign languages and complained that all the tyrants of Europe were united against him.

In July 1790, the professor was instructed, no doubt by the secret societies, to assassinate the Queen. That is why he entered the gardens of St-Cloud just as Marie-Antoinette was taking her daily walk[196]. But the rain prevented the Queen from going out that day and Rotondo does not seem to have made any other attempt.

Four months later, police reports established that an Italian "who sometimes called himself English, who was sometimes called Rotondi, sometimes Rotondo, made the most insulting remarks against the King and Queen. On 29 July 1791, he was

---

[195] *Archives nationales*, A. F'' 45 and F. 7, 4774.

[196] *Mémoires de Mme Campan*, p. 276.

prosecuted for giving money to the rioters".

"The brave Rotondo, arrested by a grenadier, was taken to the guardhouse of Henri IV's battalion where this rascal murdered him with a rifle butt to the head[197].

But Rotondo had a hard head, as four days later he was released from the Abbey prison. Arrested again for incendiary remarks, this time he spent 15 days at the Châtelet. A little later, he was returned to the Abbaye because he was accused of shooting Lafayette. M. Lenôtre pointed out that the theft of Mme du Barry's jewels coincided with the release from prison of Rotondo, who had attempted to blackmail her[198]. He was actively involved in the preparations for the days of 20 June and 10 August, and then took part in the massacres of September. Frightened, he went into hiding. Arrested in Rouen, he escaped and took refuge in Geneva, where he was arrested, carrying a large sum of money with which he had recruited a band of 200 to 300 brigands[199]. He was imprisoned after receiving, he claimed, more than fifty sabre and bayonet blows. He was then handed over to the King of Sardinia as one of the murderers of the Princesse de Lamballe and sentenced to life imprisonment. But when the French troops arrived, Rotondo was set free and obtained a passport from General Kilmaine in which he was designated as "chargé d'affaire pour la République française" ("chargé d'affaire for the French Republic"). Rotondo thought he had been saved, but on arriving in Paris he was arrested again as an agent of England, which did not prevent him from becoming a naturalized French citizen and becoming a secret agent of the Directoire. Three months later he was taken to the border by the gendarmerie. When he returned on 18 Brumaire, Napoleon had

---

[197] *L'Ami du peuple*, 29 July 1791. *Actes de la Commune*, t. VI, p. 670.

[198] Lenôtre : *Veilles maisons, vieux papiers*, 2e series, p. 149.

[199] *Actes de la Commune de Paris*, t. VI.

THE HIDDEN AUTHORS OF THE FRENCH REVOLUTION

him expelled again.

In 1811, Rotondo was again arrested in France for armed robbery, but the police simply sent him to the border. He then moved to Italy, where he was soon hanged for murder and theft[200].

Rotondo was suspected of being an agent of England and was distributing money to the rioters. So he was working for someone.

Among his friends was the Englishman Greives, who is credited with stealing Mme du Barry's jewels. Greives, who had excellent relations with Marat, had been appointed commissioner of the Committee of General Safety. By dint of denunciations against the former favourite, he obtained her arrest, accumulated all sorts of evidence against her and had all the people arrested who could have informed the justice system about the theft of the jewels. He accompanied Mme du Barry by carriage from Louveciennes to the prison. It has been wondered whether the former favourite refused to pay the price demanded for her escape, as such practices were quite widespread in the revolutionary world. Once Mme du Barry was locked up, Greives moved to the Château de Louveciennes to draw up the inventory; the municipality appointed five guards to prevent Greives from being disturbed in his work. The inventory took a long time to draw up because many valuable objects were carefully hidden. Finally, after six months, all Madame du Barry's wealth had evaporated, and Greives set off for Holland. Arrested in the middle of his journey, he was taken to the Récollets prison. But he immediately found excellent arguments to open the doors, and went to live quietly on his income in Brussels, according to M. G. Lenôtre, and in America,

---

[200] H. Furgeot: *The Marquis of St-Huruge*. G. Lenôtre : *Veilles maisons, vieux papiers,* 2ᵉ series, p. 157.

according to other authors.

Greives was one of the men who understood the practical side of the Revolution. Protected first by Mirabeau, then by Marat, he risked little by improvising as liquidator of Mme du Barry's fortune. But to prove his civic-mindedness, he founded a club in Louveciennes and had seventeen people guillotined.

Châlier, born in Suze in Piedmont, came to Paris in 1789 and became friends with Robespierre. He organised the Terror in Lyon, where he had around six thousand suspects guillotined[201], although the *Revue historique* of May 1887 states that "Châlier, a French statesman, did not kill anyone".

In one of his speeches, he said: "A sans-culotte is as invulnerable as the gods he represents on earth". Nevertheless, when the city of Lyon rose up against the terrorist regime, Châlier was guillotined in his turn on 16 July 1793.

His assistant in Lyon was Prince Charles of Hesse, whom Nodier likened to a talking tiger.

This foreigner had made rapid progress in the French army thanks to the protection of Louis XVI. However, when the courtiers at Versailles made fun of his heaviness, he declared himself a member of the revolutionary party against the party of the Court.

In all the garrisons he visited, the Prince of Hesse never ceased to denounce his superiors, comrades and subordinates. A member of the war committee declared during the Revolution: "Hesse is the most tireless of accusers, but he always disappears when it comes to providing evidence[202]. Marshal of Camp in

---

[201] *Papiers de Robespierre*, vol. II. Sybel: *Histoire de l'Europe*, vol. II, p. 347.

[202] Sybel: *Histoire de l'Europe*, t. I, p. 624.

1789, he gave speeches at the Jacobin Club in which he attacked all the generals, in particular Narbonne, Broglie, Dietrich and Montesquiou. He seems to have received a mission from the occult powers to disorganise the French armies.

When war broke out, he declared himself too ill to go to the frontier, but he was no longer ill when it came to attending meetings of the Jacobin Club. Showered with benefits by Louis XVI, he wrote to the Convention that it should condemn the tyrant to death. He edited the journal Les *Hommes libres,* and after 10 August became accustomed to signing his name "Charles Hesse, Jacobin".

Removed from office on 13 October 1793, he was soon arrested. Saved by 9 Thermidor, he tried in vain to be reinstated in the army, but was granted a retirement pension. He contributed to the most advanced newspapers. In 1798, as he was opposed to the Directoire, the police invited the Prince of Hesse to leave France. He immediately fell ill, as he did when he was fighting; then he let himself be forgotten. Arrested on 18 Brumaire, but soon released, he conspired with former Jacobins and dined with Georges Cadoudal; this time, he was interned for three years on the island of Ré. In 1803, he was deported to the German border on health grounds. He then reconciled with his family and received a pension on condition that he did not marry his mistress. At the end of the Empire, the Prince of Hesse returned to Paris; the police were quick to ask him to leave. Finally, he died in Frankfurt in 1821[203].

Among those who laughed at everything in 1789 for fear of being forced to mourn was Prince Frédéric de Salm Kirbourg, brother of the Princess of Hohenzollern. Between the Quai and the Rue de Lille, he had built the palace that is now the

---

[203] Chuquet: *Un Prince Jacobin.* Sybel: *History of Europe*, t. I.

Chancellery of the Legion of Honour[204].

Appointed marshal of camp, he shone less on the battlefield than in the salons. He was in Utrecht with eight thousand men when he learned of the arrival of the Germans; he immediately decamped without a fight and returned to Paris to amuse himself. Appointed by Lafayette as a battalion commander in the National Guard, the Prince of Salm made a fool of himself with his revolutionary zeal[205].

His palace was a meeting place for the most opinionated constituents. However, he was unable to forget his birth and was guillotined as an aristocrat.

Dubuisson, a mediocre poet and unsuccessful author, was of Belgian origin[206]. A member of the Paris Commune insurrection committee and vice-president of the Jacobin club, he managed to get some of his plays performed at the Montansier theatre.

As an emissary of the Jacobin club, he went with two other foreigners, Proly and Péreyra, to ask Dumouriez to account for his threats against the Convention.

According to Robespierre, Dubuisson and Proly, covered by the mask of sans-culottism, organised a system of counter-revolution and had English, Prussian and Austrian bankers as accomplices. Nevertheless, Dubuisson was one of the foreigners employed by our Ministry of Foreign Affairs in 1793. Charged with a secret mission in Switzerland, he ended up being proscribed at the same time as Hébert and was guillotined in

---

[204] Put up for lottery after the Prince's conviction, this hotel was bought by a wigmaker's boy, Lieuthraud, who also bought the Château de Bagatelle.

[205] Fr. Masson. *Joséphine de Beauharnais*, p. 186.

[206] *Memoirs of Durand de Maillane*. Taine: *La Révolution*, etc.

1794.

The Italian Dufourny was a member of the Commune's revolutionary committee and president of the Paris department. He was a regular member of the Committee of General Safety and attended all the deliberations of the Committee of Public Safety. His zeal even seemed suspicious to his colleagues. Robespierre pointed out that Dufourny had infiltrated the insurrection committee on 31 May; "when he saw that the movement was going to succeed, he sought ways to render it impotent".

A very active member of the Cordeliers and the Jacobins, Dufourny was proscribed by Robespierre for having defended Danton. The 9th of Thermidor saved his life; he was then arrested again as an agent of foreigners, and amnestied on the 4th of Brumaire, year IV. He became administrator of powders and saltpetre.

François Robert[207], a journalist from Liège, married Mlle de Kéralio. A friend of Danton, protected by Mme Roland, a member of the Jacobins and Cordeliers clubs, he was elected deputy for Paris. The first republican group was formed in his salon. Editor of the *Mercure* and *Révolutions de Paris,* François Robert formed a central committee to unite the popular societies of Paris.

Fearing arrest in 1791, he went into hiding at Roland's house; later he drew up an indictment against the household that had given him hospitality.

On 22 June 1792, on the proposal of François Robert, the Club des Cordeliers voted an address to the National Assembly calling for the establishment of the Republic. It argued to the Convention

---

[207] He should not be confused with François Robert, a French geographer.

that every Frenchman had the right to assassinate Louis XVI.

Brissot had promised him an embassy (Petersburg, Vienna or Warsaw); Dumouriez's influence caused this bizarre choice to fail. To compensate him, Danton took him on as secretary to the ministry of justice.

Suddenly rich in 1793, François Robert paid off his debts and gave luxurious dinners.

Included in the trial of the revolutionary committee of the Social Contract, he was sentenced on 8 August 1795: I° to degradation by the state, 2° to be tied in a straitjacket for two hours[208]. François Robert was no longer mentioned. He was exiled in 1816.

Joseph Gorani, a famous Milanese literary scholar, was a friend of Voltaire and d'Holbach. As early as 1770, his *Traité du despotisme* set out clearly revolutionary theories. In correspondence with the main leaders of the 1789 movement, he gradually made friends with the most exalted Jacobins. Settling in Paris at the beginning of 1792, he wrote violent articles against Louis XVI and apologies for the Revolution in several newspapers, notably the *Moniteur,* which were later published in a volume entitled *Lettres aux souverains sur la Révolution Française (Letters to the Sovereigns on the French Revolution).*

Bailly granted Gorani the title of French citizen in recognition of the services he had rendered to the cause of liberty. Nevertheless, after 9 Thermidor, Gorani thought it wiser to leave France. But he was exiled and stripped of his possessions by Archduke Ferdinand "for having behaved badly in Paris"; he then

---

[208] Aulard: *Histoire politique de la Révolution Française,* pp. 86 ff, 135 ff. Aulard : *Paris sous la réaction Thermidorienne.* Aulard: *Études sur la Révolution* (3e series).

took refuge in Geneva and was never heard from again.

Gorani enjoyed a satisfaction rarely accorded to literati: when word of his death spread in 1804, he was able to read his funeral oration and a few obituaries praising his works. He died only fifteen years later.

F. Ch. Laukhard, son of a German pastor, successively professor at the University of Halle and soldier, left the German army to join the revolutionary army. In Lyon, his battalion formed the escort of honour near the guillotine. Arrested during the Terror, released on 9 Thermidor, Laukhard returned to Germany and enlisted in the emigrant army to earn ten louis, then immediately deserted to become a teacher again. He died an alcoholic.

The Italian Buonarotti had problems with his country's police and settled in Corsica in 1789. He was expelled because of his revolutionary writings. He returned in 1792 as commissioner of the executive power at the court of Corte; the commune of Toulon awarded him a certificate of good citizenship. An excellent musician, he claimed to be descended from Michelangelo; it was probably Freemasonry that launched him into revolutionary circles. A member of the Jacobin club, he was one of Robespierre's most frequent guests, who appointed him as the Convention's commissioner for the Italian armies in 1794.

Buonarotti was arrested with Babeuf, despite Carnot's protection, and deported to Pelée Island near Cherbourg, then to Oléron, and finally to Elba. In 1806 he obtained permission to settle in Geneva under police surveillance; there, with Marat's brother, he founded a Masonic lodge, the *Amis sincères,* affiliated to the Philadelphes. After 1815, he founded the *Sublimes Maîtres Parfaits* group. Expelled from Geneva in 1823, he went to preach socialism in Brussels.

After 1830 Buonarotti returned to France and took an active

part in revolutionary agitation. M. Mathiez considers him one of the founders of the socialist party in France[209].

Cérutti, originally from Turin, was a great friend of Mirabeau. He worked with Rabaud St Etienne on the *Feuille villageoise*. He did enough for the revolutionary cause to have the street now known as rue Laffitte named after him. Cérutti must not have been very bloodthirsty, judging by his works: *Poëme sur le jeu des échecs, Apologie de l'Ordre des Jésuites, Oraison funèbre de Mirabeau,* etc...

The Venezuelan Miranda owed his rapid advancement in the French army at the start of the Revolution to British protection: Pétion and Brissot admitted as much.

He had very advanced opinions: it was he who denounced his general-in-chief, Dumouriez, to the Convention. His attitude at Neerwinde appeared suspicious to several officers and was described as treason[210] without any proof. Robespierre declared in April 1793: "Stengel, a German aristocrat, and Miranda, a Spanish adventurer employed by Pitt, betrayed us at the same time in Aix-la-Chapelle and Maastricht". However, Miranda was acquitted and crowned with flowers. Shortly afterwards he was arrested again as a friend of the Girondins. Released on 9 Thermidor, he was proscribed on 18 Fructidor and took refuge in England. Some time later Miranda was found in Paris; he was arrested on the occasion of the infernal machine attack. As soon as he was released, he thought it prudent to settle in America. Returning to Paris under the Consulate, he was expelled by the police as an agent of Pitt. In America, he founded a Masonic

[209] A. Mathiez: *Études Robespierristes*, t. I. Robiquet: *Buonarotti*. Hamel: *Histoire de Robespierre,* p. 298 ff.

[210] *Mémoires de Thibaudeau*, t. I, p. 14. See also de Pradt: *Histoire de la Belgique.*

lodge where this minister passed on his advice through Miranda.

Salicetti denounced him as an agent of England; according to the Duchesse d'Abrantès, Napoleon Ier believed him to be a spy for both Spain and England[211].

Miranda died in prison in Cadiz in 1816[212].

Frédéric Gentz, the author of revolutionary pamphlets, had put his pen to the fairly well-paid service of Prussia, England and Austria. At the age of sixty he fell madly in love with Fanny Essler, and his passion for the famous artist earned Gentz a certain notoriety[213].

Rebmann, a German journalist affiliated with the Illuminati, settled in Paris at the start of the Revolution and joined the judiciary.

Can we count Lebrun Tondu among the foreigners? It's debatable. The dictionaries tell us that Lebrun, a French statesman, was born in Noyon. However, all foreigners who took part in the Revolution are generally described as French statesmen. It is impossible to find any trace of Lebrun's family in Noyon, and some of his contemporaries said that he was from Liège[214]. He was in turn a clergyman, soldier, deserter, printer, tutor in Belgium, mathematician and journalist. The Girondins felt that the exercise of so many different professions was a good preparation for a career as a minister; they entrusted him with the portfolio of foreign affairs, then the Ministry of War.

---

[211] *Mémoires de la Duchesse d'Abrantès*, t. I, p. 290.

[212] O'Kelly de Galway: *Miranda*.

[213] André Beaunier: *Faces of women*.

[214] Sybel: *Histoire de l'Europe*, p. 445, t. I.

When he was living in Liège, Lebrun Tondu, who had made a successful start in journalism, entered into talks with the Austrian government, which offered to take him on in return for one hundred pistols a year. But Lebrun nobly refused to sell his pen for less than a hundred louis a year[215]. Once in power he showed himself to be rather moderate, conspiring with Dumouriez and trying to save Louis XVI. Was it for this reason that he was guillotined in December 1793, or for having instructed Desfieux to intercept Jacobin dispatches[216]. History does not say.

Can Hassenfratz, described as a German chemist by several authors[217], also be considered French? One of the most violent members of the Commune, Hassenfratz was first clerk to Pache, Minister of War; he had previously gone bankrupt under another name. Appointed supplier to the armies, he was thus able to re-establish his finances.

Hassenfratz edited the *Journal des Sciences;* under the Empire he became a professor at the Ecole Polytechnique.

J. Conrad de Cock, editor of the *Sans-culotte Batave,* has two places of residence, not counting Holland; in Passy he is an aristocrat and gives dinner parties where people drink wine offered, it is said, by the English government. In central Paris he was a revolutionary and a member of Hébert's section. Guillotinated during the Terror, he left a son more famous than him, Paul de Cock, who claims to have saved his mother, at the age of ten months, by smiling at Fouquier Tinville[218]. But Paul

---

[215] *Correspondence of W. A. Miles*, p. 34.

[216] See above, page 100.

[217] Among others Reichardt: *Un Prussien en France*, p. 190.

[218] Leroux Cesbron: *Gens et choses d'autrefois.*

de Cock had a vivid imagination!

Westermann claimed that Conrad de Cock and his friends had sacrificed 420,000 pounds for the cause of freedom.

The German shoemaker Wilcheritz, a friend of Robespierre, was administrator of the Luxembourg prison; perpetually drunk, he was guillotined after 9 Thermidor.

In 1789, it was another German who presided over the looting of Strasbourg's town hall [219] : Chrétien Vollmar, son of the coachman to the Elector of Mainz, was the first to jump into the citadel conquered by the riot. One of his fellow citizens, named Weber, was a depositary of seditious pamphlets and helped to spread them; the police seized a large number of them from his home on 8 January 1790.

Pio, a Neapolitan and former chargé d'affaires to the King of the Two Sicilies, contributed to the *Journal de la Montagne and* was employed at the Hôtel de Ville as "commissaire pour les papiers des émigrés". He then ran the passport office, a highly lucrative position during the period of proscription. Finally, he joined the Ministry of Foreign Affairs. Pio was a member of the Club des Bons Enfants. According to Nicolas de Bonneville, he received money from foreign courts and inspired Marat's articles and Robespierre's speeches[220].

A Dutchman, Pastor Maron, a friend of Ronsin, dedicated the Protestant temple in Paris to his country.

The Belgian Gœmars denounces the monarchists to the Committee of General Safety.

---

[219] *Revue historique*. December 1915 (Article by Mr R. Reuss).

[220] A. Mathiez : *La Révolution et les étrangers*, page 134.

The American Smith was sent to Basel by the Comité de Salut Public on a financial mission.

His fellow citizen Oswald left his young wife at the start of the Revolution to fight in France under the flag of liberty, and wrote numerous revolutionary pamphlets in verse and prose. He was appointed colonel of artillery and, on Paine's recommendation, was given a secret mission to Ireland [221]. Oswald was one of the founders of the *Chronique du Mois, a* Girondin newspaper. During a stay in India, he converted to Buddhism; he gave vegetarian dinners that astonished Parisians.

The German Creutz, better known as Curtius, had founded a museum of wax figures, which was very popular with elegant society. Curtius was one of the victors of the Bastille.

Mayor Fleuriol was from Brussels. J.-Ch-F. Hoffmann, born in Kosteim near Mainz, became a lieutenant colonel in our national guard. The Swiss P.-E.-J. de Rivaz was also a lieutenant colonel. The Genoese F.-I. Sauter was appointed general in 1793[222].

The Silesian E. Oelsner, a confidant of Sieyès and linked with the leaders of the Constituent Assembly, was a correspondent of Archenholz's *Minerva*[223]. His friend Halem, of German origin, settled in France in 1790 and attended meetings of the Jacobins and the Cercle Social. His fellow citizen, Professor I.-H. Campe, moved to Paris after the Fourteenth of July, giving up his position as director of the Philanthropinum in Dessau, a famous educational establishment. He took his pupil William de Humbolt with him and wrote enthusiastic panegyrics on the

---

[221] *Foreign Affairs Archives.* London, V. 587.

[222] G. Dumont: *Battalions of national volunteers in 1791.*

[223] *Annales révolutionnaires.* April 1918. Albert Mathiez : *Pilgrims to freedom.*

French Revolution.

The Swiss Devalot donated 6,000 pounds to the revolutionary movement. The notable people of Genoa offered 900,000 pounds to the Constituent Assembly.

While the English poet Wordsworth was frequenting the clubs, his fellow countryman Astley set up an equestrian amphitheatre on Boulevard du Temple. The Chaumières ball belonged to the Englishman Tinkson.

The composer Reichardt, director of the Berlin Opera, came to Paris in 1791 and 1792 and expressed his admiration for the revolutionary movement.

The Bavarian Merck, a lieutenant in the Austrian army, joined the French army in November 1792. The American J.-K. Eustace fought in the Vendée wars and obtained the rank of marshal de camp. The Spaniard Marchena collaborated with Marat, conspired with Miranda, then turned to the royalist side, having worked on Girondist propaganda with his fellow Spaniard Hevia, a former embassy secretary.

Prince Stroganof worked for the revolution under the name of Otcher. Secretary of the *Friends of the Law* Club, he attended meetings of the Jacobins[224].

Jaubert, a Belgian officer in the service of Austria, joins the revolutionary police. Among others, he denounced his fellow Belgian, the banker Herries, employed by Pitt in Paris. He claimed that by also searching Walkiers and Langendongue, bankers in Brussels, it would be easy to prove their relations with the English government.

---

[224] A. Mathiez : *La Révolution et les étrangers*, p. 28.

The Germans Cotta, Dorsch, G. Kerner, Wedekind, etc., met in the rue de la Jussienne, under the chairmanship of the explorer G. Forster, to discuss politics. The Genoese Grenus, a friend of Proly, was in correspondence with the agents of the Austrian government. Count Poroni, who had come from Italy to make revolutionary propaganda in Paris, was denounced to the Convention as a foreign agent; he then suddenly disappeared and returned to his country.

His fellow citizen Marino, a Commune police officer, was "driven by a real thirst for blood[225]". He was arrested at the same time as Hébert and Dobsen.

Is it by chance that so many foreigners have gathered in Paris to change the form of French government? Or is there not a plan skilfully organised by an occult power? Obscure mercenaries manoeuvre under the orders of intelligent leaders. We remember the leading role played by the Marseillais battalion in the attack on the Tuileries. Was it, as M. Aulard writes, made up of young men from good families? Judging from their attitude and actions, this is quite improbable. Taine, Blanc Gilly, L. Lautard, etc., state that this battalion comprised 516 adventurers selected one by one, Spaniards, Italians, Levantines, whose mayor, Mouraille, was quite happy to relieve the burden of Marseilles. At the same time, Peyron went to Geneva to recruit the twelve most famous terrorists of that republic and bring them to Paris[226]. Once their work was done, on 10 August, they wanted to send these terrible soldiers to the border, but they declared that they preferred to return to Marseille. In the presence of this courage, the Council of Ministers voted to congratulate them on their patriotism and bravery (meeting of 14 September 1792).

In the Vendée War, the Republican armies contained a large

---

[225] A. Schmidt: *Paris during the Revolution*, according to secret police reports.

[226] General Danican: *The brigands unmasked.*

number of "Belgians, Batavians, Negroes and adventurers expelled from their countries for crimes"[227]. In Nantes in 1793, the troop known as the American Hussars was made up of negroes and mulattoes. They were given women to shoot and used them for their own pleasure. In the Vendée, the German legion shot women in groups of twenty-five and finished them off with rifle butts[228]. For such a task the government of the Republic feared it would not find any Frenchmen!

At Quiberon, according to Allonville's secret memoirs, the Republican soldiers refused to shoot the unarmed prisoners to whom they had promised their lives. So they called in Belgians[229].

Isn't it consoling for French people of all parties to be able to blame foreigners for most of the crimes that dishonour the Revolution!

A number of police officers were employed as "sheep", i.e. they acted as agents provocateurs in prisons, getting prisoners to gossip and then denouncing them. This job was generally given to foreigners[230].

Not only did they occupy the galleries of our assemblies, but they mingled with the deputies, so that one wondered if they were not voting at the same time as them. When Malouet once proposed that important deliberations should be held in camera, Volney replied:

"Foreigners have the right to see and hear everything so they

---

[227] *Mémoires de Puisaye*, p. 411.

[228] Taine: *La Révolution Française*, vol. III, p. 376 ff.

[229] L. Gastinne: *La belle Tallien*.

[230] *Mémoires de Mlle de Coigny* (introduction).

can assess whether we are staying true to our mandate."

At the end of September 1790, the foreigners were ordered to withdraw from the Assembly, but they found ways of not always obeying.

The government itself was invaded by foreigners. While the Terror was being organised in Paris by the Swiss Marat, in Lyon by the Italian Châlier and in Strasbourg by the German Schneider, the Swiss occupied the Ministry of War, the Paris City Hall and the Ministry of Finance. Once in power, Pache set up the purchasing department, responsible for all military supplies; the directors were the Swiss Bidermann and Marx Beer, son of a Jew well known for his swindles. The agents were Simon Pick and Mosselniann (from Brussels), Perlan and Carpentier (from Ostend), and the Cerf Beer brothers. This was the beginning of the disorganisation of the army. As some critics have questioned the evidence I have given of this disorganisation (in the history of General Dumouriez), I would point them to the recent volume by M. A. Chuquet on Dumouriez[231].

The Swiss Castella was then in the offices of the Ministry of War; his compatriot Niquille was a clerk on the Committee of General Safety.

The Minister of Foreign Affairs claimed to be French, but many people accused him of being Belgian; in any case, among our diplomats in 1794 were the English spy Baldwin, the Italian swindler Rotondo, the Prussian Forster, the Swiss Jeanneret and Schweitzer, the Englishman Thomas Christie, the Belgian Dubuisson, the American Oswald, the German Reinhard, the Swiss J.-I. Clavière (from Geneva), brother of the Minister of Finance, the Prussian Cloots and the Austrian Proly. The Belgian Robert would have had, without the protests of Dumouriez, the

---

[231] A. Chuquet: *Dumouriez*, pages 150 et seq.

embassy of Vienna or Petersburg. Pereira received in Brumaire year II, a mission of the ministry for Foreign Affairs in the North of France.

Bidermann from Genoa was treasurer of the Ministry of Foreign Affairs. Fortunately, the ambassadors' introducer was a Frenchman, Pigeot, a former notary previously sentenced to twenty years hard labour.

The foreign revolutionaries were so at home in Paris that they had come to believe they were French. Marat once said to General Ward: "The French are mad to let foreigners live in their homes; we should cut off their ears, let them bleed for a few days and then cut off their heads[232]. General Ward then timidly pointed out that Marat himself was a foreigner.

The majority of French politicians had ties with the cosmopolitan syndicate that ran events. Thus, Chabot was a puppet whose strings were held by the spies Emmanuel and Junius Frey. Brissot, who owed money to everyone in London, wrote for the *Courrier de l'Europe,* owned by the Englishman Swinton. Rewbel is the businessman of two German Princes. Basire's mistress was Mme d'Aelders, a secret agent of the Prussian government. Noël, a friend of Danton and Inspector General of Public Education, is the son-in-law of a Belgian banker. Drouin is an agent of the Prince of Wittemberg. Hérault de Séchelles was the lover of the sister of an Austrian officer and betrayed the secrets of the Committee of Public Safety to Austria[233]. Westermann, who had twice been expelled from Paris for theft, was said to have been bought by the Prussian government[234]. Soulavie, a diplomatic agent in Switzerland,

---

[232] Conway: *Paine* (*Rabbe* 1900), p. 277.

[233] *Robespierre's notes for St-Just's report. Hamel: Robespierre,* t. III, p. 453.

[234] L. Madelin: *La Révolution.* See session of the Convention, 23rd December 1792. Biré: *Journal d'un bourgeois de Paris,* t. II, p. 126.

wrote to Robespierre that "a very good patriot reports Kellermann as sold to the Emperor[235]".

Rabaut St-Etienne admitted that the Jacobins were under foreign influence. He wrote at the time of the Champ de Mars massacre: "We cannot hide the fact that money was spread and that the seditious influence came from outside[236].

Robespierre accused Lebrun Tondu of being sold out to Austria while Brissot was sold out to England. But the Committee of Public Safety accused so many people that it was sometimes mistaken. Thus we find a declaration stating that Hoche was a traitor. This denunciation was signed by Collot d'Herbois, Robespierre, Carnot, Billaud-Varenne and Barère.

The annales révolutionnaires of July 1914 reported an accusation, accompanied by precise details, against the Conventionnel Antoine Guerber; Gugenthal, a former Prussian officer who had gone over to the service of France, asserted that Guerber sent letters to Professor Weber in Strasbourg intended for Generals Wurmser and Kalgstein; the Prussians and Austrians were thus kept informed of everything that was happening at the Convention. Vadier, president of the Convention and of the Committee of General Safety, stated that Fabre d'Églantine was Pitt's main agent[237].

We'll come back to this point later.

---

[235] *Papiers de Robespierre.* Buchez et Roux, t. XXXV, p. 383.

[236] *Correspondence of Rabaut St-Étienne. French Revolution*, volume XXXV. Letter of 17 July 1791. A. Mathiez : *La Révolution et les étrangers*, p. 121.

[237] A. Tournier: *Vadier, Chairman of the Committee of General Safety*, p. 110.

CHAPTER VII

AUSTRIA

In 1789, France and Austria were allies, but while the ruling families maintained friendly relations, the Austrian statesmen were anti-French. France, in the "sunset of the monarchy", was an obstacle to the plans of almost all the powers, and in particular to the partition of Poland. Kaunitz, who hated our country, was, according to Gustave Bord, the promoter of the alliance because he "hoped to benefit Austria alone. His successor Thugut had a blind hatred of France[238].

The death of Joseph II loosened the ties between the two monarchies. Mercy Argenteau wrote to Kaunitz at[239]: "The new monarch and the queen hardly know each other, and they have always shown little liking for each other. Marie-Antoinette had not seen her brother since the age of ten.

In 1789, Austria appeared to be a complete stranger to the revolutionary movement; the only Austrian to take an active part in the events was Kaunitz's natural son, Count Proly (or Prohli)[240]. The Freys were more Israelites than Austrians, and their role could be explained by Freemasonry. Nevertheless, it is

---

[238] G. Bord: *Autour du Temple*, t. I, p. 134 ff.

[239] 10th March 1790.

[240] His name is sometimes spelt Proli.

more or less proven that they were spies in the service of Austria; they were probably also bribed by Prussia[241].

At the beginning of the troubles, fomented by England and Prussia, as we shall prove later, Austrian policy could hardly have been revolutionary. Mercy Argenteau was outraged by the campaign against Marie-Antoinette. It is impossible," he wrote, "to pinpoint the causes of the frenzy that has seized people's minds against the Queen. The absurdities attributed to her, to which common sense is repugnant, cannot be the only reason. There must be some secret cabal behind it.

Mercy Argenteau soon pointed out to the Emperor that France, preoccupied with its internal dissensions, would not be able to intervene in European affairs for long. The Austrian government remained Louis XVI's ally solely in order to have a free hand in Poland and Turkey. It was said in Vienna that if the Emperor followed his inclination, he would "supply ten thousand men to a democratic army and as many to an aristocratic army[242].

But in 1792, the alliance was broken and war declared. From then on, Austria wanted to save the royal family and above all to stifle the revolutionary fervour that could spread to neighbouring countries. Mercy, who had always been a friend of France, drew up a dismemberment project in which Austria's share would be as follows: The Netherlands would be extended as far as the Somme. From the source of this river, the border would join the Meuse at Sedan or Mézières. Alsace and Lorraine would return to the Empire. France would be "reduced to impotence for the rest of the centuries"[243].

---

[241] Vicomte de Bonald, F. Chabot: *Archives nationales*, F. 7, 4637.

[242] *Foreign Affairs Archives*, Vienna, v. 362.

[243] *Correspondence of Mercy Argenteau, published by Flammermont. Letters to Thugut*, 15 June and 12 July 1793.

The aggravation of our disorders thus served the plans of the Vienna cabinet and it favoured them, albeit with less activity than Prussia and England.

The role of Proly, the natural son of Kaunitz[244], remains rather enigmatic: Why did he settle in Paris, like so many foreigners in 1789, and did he associate with the leading Jacobinists[245]? Initially lodging with the Frey family, Proly introduced himself into the committees, collaborated with Barère and Hérault de Séchelles, and gave his opinion in the offices of the Minister of Foreign Affairs[246]. He advised Lebrun Tondu and was entrusted by him with various diplomatic missions. He founded about fifty popular clubs. Robespierre said at the Jacobins Club (November 1793): "Proly's aim is to upset everything and lose the Jacobins. He is impregnable, as are his main accomplices, who are above all English, Prussian and Austrian bankers".

Having made some successful speculations on the Stock Exchange, Proly led a happy life. After the death of Louis XVI, he turned to the counter-revolutionaries. A pleasure companion, the Comte de Champgrand, introduced him to Jean de Batz, and Proly joined the famous conspirator's gang. He then simulated a trade in paintings with Champgrand. Nevertheless, in March 1793, just as Dumouriez was beginning to threaten the Convention, Proly was sent with Pereyra and Dubuisson to ask the general to account for his attitude. Marat declared that he had well deserved his country. But on 9 Nivôse an II, Proly was arrested. Elusive at home, he spent his evenings playing at Mme de Ste-Amaranthe's house.

"The most exact search was carried out in this house, say the

---

[244] His mother was a first cousin of Anarchasis Cloots.

[245] He then founded a newspaper, Le *Cosmopolite*.

[246] Buchez et Roux: *Histoire parlementaire*, t. XXXI, p. 375 et seq. Avenel: *Anarchasis Cloots*.

agents of the Committee of Public Safety; we found nothing relevant to our mission. The citizen Ste-Amaranthe declared that she knew Proly neither directly nor indirectly[247]". The seals are placed in the flat in the rue des Fille St-Thomas, lent or rented by Desfieux to Proly. On 18 Nivôse, the surveillance committee voted 200 livres to cover the costs incurred in the search for Batz's accomplice. After a long pursuit, two members of the search committee entered the au berge du Petit-Cerf, in Vandereau (Seine-et-Oise), on 30 Pluviôse, to freshen up and discovered Proly disguised as a cook. Kaunitz's son was immediately arrested and taken to La Force prison. Hérault de Séchelles tearfully demanded the freedom of his accomplice; in fact Proly, who, it is said, had been informed by Hérault de Séchelles of everything that was happening at the Public Safety Committee[248], passed on the news to the Austrian government.

His intervention failed, but Collot d'Herbais was more skilful and obtained the release of Proly, Desfieux and Rutledge, agents of England (October 1793)[249]. Arrested a second time a few months later, Proly was sentenced to death on 24 March 1794.

The national archives have carefully preserved the slips establishing Proly's speculations on shares in the Red Sea, the Compagnie des Indes, etc., but there is no trace of his political correspondence.

The Austrian government's talks with Dumouriez during the Belgian campaign are well known. The Viennese court later entered into secret negotiations with Robespierre through Montgaillard. Barthélemy's papers attest to this but do not reveal

[247] *Archives nationales,* F. 7, 2774.

[248] Hamel: *Histoire de Robespierre*, p. 453.

[249] A. Mathiez: *Was Hérault de Séchelles a Dantonist* (*Annales révolutionnaires*, July 1914).

any details[250]. As for Montgaillard's memoirs, they are somewhat suspect as they sometimes distort the truth. But there is reason to believe that Mongaillard was Robespierre's representative when he was received by François II in April 1794. M. Cl. de Lacroix[251] observed that "very powerful motives were needed to determine the emperor to receive a person whose rank and origins must have seemed suspicious to him". It was around the same time that the Incorruptible came into contact with Louis XVIII's emissaries[252]. Perhaps there is a link between these various negotiations.

After the death of Louis XVI, Austria made common cause with Europe in the fight against the Revolution. Hirsinger's confidences and the correspondence of Jeanneret, the diplomatic agent in Switzerland, provide proof that the Vienna cabinet had "men in France so skilful that they are believed to be the most zealous republicans. Exaggeration after exaggeration will lead to the goal of destroying the Convention by the people and by itself by dividing it. The Constitutionalists were destroyed by the Girondins, and then the Girondins were driven to ruin. To bring down this party and that of Orléans, the Vienna cabinet made the most astonishing sacrifices"[253].

This is exactly the tactic used by Jean de Batz.

Minister Thugut said: "What is essential is that there are parties in France that fight and weaken each other"[254].

---

[250] *Letter from Barthélemy to Buchot,* 30 August 1794.

[251] *Souvenirs* of the *Count of Montgaillard* published by Cl. de LACROIX.

[252] *Revue de la Révolution.* 1888, p. 194. Article by M. G. BORD.

[253] *Barthélemy's papers. Letter from Jeanneret to Deforgues.* 19th February 1794.

[254] Sorel, vol. III, p. 329.

In short, Austria should not be counted among the hidden authors of the French Revolution, but it is actively working for the counter-revolution. However, its indifference towards the unfortunate prisoners of the Temple[255] is surprising.

---

[255] See on this point: Ménard: *Histoire du Directoire* and Comte d'Hérisson: *Autour d'une Révolution.*

CHAPTER VIII

PRUSSIA

The French have often deluded themselves about Europe's feelings towards them: they thought they were admired and loved when they were merely envied. The infatuation of our philosophers with Prussia in the eighteenth century is the result of one of these illusions. Frederick II flattered them because they were preparing the Revolution that Europe wanted.

The alliance between the two great Catholic nations displeased the Protestant powers. Prussia wanted to expand in Germany and was plotting to divide up Poland, which was protected by France. By intervening in our affairs, Prussia perhaps had a third aim: to replace Louis XVI with the Duke of Brunswick.

The Berlin cabinet decided that the easiest way to put France at odds with Austria was to arouse public opinion in Paris against Marie-Antoinette. This role was entrusted to the Jew Ephraim, of whom we will speak a little later. As the Marquis de Moustiers observed, behind Ephraim was the ambassador Von der Goltz, whom Mirabeau described as "shrewd, cunning, very personal and greedy; money was his dominant passion".

Several years before the Revolution, Vergennes had already warned Louis XVI that Baron de Goltz was the head of Prussian espionage. Charged by his sovereign with breaking up

Louis XVI's household, Goltz had tried unsuccessfully to provide the king with a mistress [256]. Having failed in this negotiation, he fuelled public opinion against Marie-Antoinette, subsidised revolutionary newspapers in Paris and distributed money to French politicians[257].

Freemasonry had prepared the ground to accept German influence. In 1789, the movement was well underway and spirits were aroused against the "Austrians". The day after the Bastille was taken by bands of mostly Germans, Von der Goltz considered 14 July to be a victory for Prussia[258]. From time to time, in Berlin, he read articles paid for by him in newspapers supporting the new ideas, and proved that "Prussia, thanks to its generous diplomacy, can be considered the best protector of the Revolution" [259]. Camille Desmoulins, in his history of the Brissotins, claimed that the right side of the Convention was run by an Anglo-Prussian committee. He pointed out the following statement by Phélippeaux: "The expenses of the King of Prussia last year (1792), count six million ecus for corruptions in France"[260].

Barère also told the Convention "The movement we are threatened with belongs to London, Madrid and Berlin"[261].

Only two played an important role, Ephraim and Anacharsis Cloots, who claimed to be estranged from his country.

---

[256] P. d'ESTRÉE: *The great master of espionage. (Nouvelle Revue,* 15 February 1918).

[257] *Archives nationales,* A. F" 45.

[258] *Correspondence of Von der Goltz,* published by Flammermont, p. 130.

[259] See the article by Mr G. Gautherot in the *Universe of* 4 November 1913.

[260] Buchez and Roux. *Parliamentary History,* t. XXVI, p. 289.

[261] Id. t. XXVII. Session of 31 May.

Ephraim centralised the whole conspiracy against Marie-Antoinette; he launched the first pamphlets against her, after having collaborated successfully in the affair of the necklace. An agent of the Rose Croix Freemasons, he had been introduced to the French political world by the ambassador Von der Goltz, who introduced him to the Constitutionalists and then to the Girondins. Little by little, Éphraïm became friends with Marat, St-Huruge, Carra, Rotondo and Gorsas; he frequented the clubs and was extremely violent. The Marquis de Moustiers, ambassador to Berlin, wrote: "There is nothing that Ephraim will not say against the Queen; I am fairly certain that he is spreading money around and I know that he receives considerable sums from bankers".

Fersen wrote to Gustav III: "It is not long since Ephraim received 600,000 pounds, which he provides for revolutionary propaganda"[262]. It was well known in Paris that Ephraim was a secret agent of the Berlin government, since diplomatic correspondence informed the French ambassador that "Madame Ephraim will facilitate the means for him to see Bischofswerder and even the King of Prussia[263].

In 1790, the Berlin cabinet was so pleased with Ephraim's services that it appointed him to the embassy with the apparent mission of looking after trade affairs. The skilful Israelite soon wrote to Berlin: "The first members of the National Assembly are so inclined towards Prussian friendship that one could ask for anything at this moment". A little later he added: "The Jacobin club is completely devoted to Prussia"[264].

Is the explanation for this great sympathy to be found in the letter in which Éphraïm speaks of the sums sent by the Prussian

---

[262] See G. Bord. *La conspiration révolutionnaire de 1789*, p. 191.

[263] *Foreign Affairs Archives.* Berlin, 1790.

[264] Correspondence with Von der Goltz, p. 133.

government to Choderlos de Laclos, Philippe Égalité's right-hand man? It is worth quoting the main passages of this letter, which proves: I° that the leaders of the Revolution were bribed by the King of Prussia; 2° that by demanding reforms it was hoped that Louis XVI would refuse them, thus aggravating the revolutionary effervescence.

Ephraim to Laclos, 22 April 1791[265]:

"I've been told that you're desperate because you've missed out on your last venture. I think so, it cost us a lot of money, and in these times you can't spare it too much. Such, at least, are the intentions of my master King Frederick William...

I had counted that the King would not suddenly dismiss the priests from his chapel and that, by doing so, we would still find some way to make people shout at him. Not at all, he dismisses them, and we are still the dupes. This man is impregnable; from whichever side you attack him, he suddenly disarms you. Who would have calculated to find on the throne a man who sacrifices all his personal pleasures to the tranquillity of his people?

The decrees still left some gentlemen of the chamber. We had already arranged to cause another good riot. I thought we could succeed with that; he anticipated the blow, he sent his gentlemen away and left us short with all our plans.

Our situation was brilliant for a few hours, I even thought that your kind boss would replace his cousin; but now my hopes are no longer the same... All I like about it is that we have lost Lafayette in this shock, and that's already a lot.

Our 500,000 francs are consumed more or less uselessly, that is what I find most unfortunate; we will not have such sums at

---

[265] *Bibliothèque nationale*, L. b. 39, 9888.

our disposal every day and the King of Prussia will tire of providing the money… We must arm ourselves with courage, wait for what the couriers we have sent to all the departments have done. If, on the contrary, they have achieved nothing, I think we will have to give up the game…

P.S. I hear that the Guards don't want to let their general go. This blow is devastating… Hurry up and assemble the council and let me know what time it is.

It was only in January 1791 that the French government appeared to be concerned about Ephraim's activities. A letter, written entirely in the hand of M. de Montmorin, instructed the Marquis de Moustiers to carry out an investigation in Berlin into this worrying Israelite who "seems to have been sent here to intrigue in the most criminal manner… I have been told things about him that I will not allow myself to report because they are too atrocious… This intriguer has sought to make friends with people whose ardour for the Revolution makes them more likely to listen to him. His aim was to compromise us with the Emperor; he thought that by arousing the spirits against the Queen he could achieve this more easily"[266].

Moustier could think of nothing better for this investigation than to go and question Mrs Ephraim, which at first sight seems rather naive. He admits (10 February 1791) that he was unable to get her to talk. However, she said in conversation that if Bischofswerder was far away, she would not know to whom to give her husband's letters to the King of Prussia.

In response to further complaints from M. de Montmorin, the Marquis de Moustiers replied on 28 February: "Éphraïm has a reputation here as an intriguer who is always ready to be disowned". Finally, on 13 April, he wrote: "I cannot escape the

---

[266] *Foreign Affairs Archives.* Berlin, c. 212.

suspicion that the Prussian court has long been intent on stirring up trouble among us…

I know from his wife's confession that Ephraim has boasted of rendering great services to the king; that he has feared on several occasions to run great risks…

If we were inclined to believe evil on the basis of appearances, we might believe it to be authorised to act as it does…".

Unfortunately, Louis XVI's entourage did not easily believe in evil, nor did his officials. Moutiers therefore concluded by rejecting the idea that Ephraim had acted on the orders of his government [267] . He then proposed a Franco-Prussian rapprochement, in order to thwart England's perfidious manoeuvres[268]. This time he saw clearly, suspecting England of leading events.

By this time, the French court was so disarmed that Marie-Antoinette asked Blumendorf to get Kaunitz to contact the King of Prussia in order to stop Ephraim's machinations. So we read in the diplomatic correspondence of Moustiers (26 May)

"The Count of Goltz must have told Ephraim to be more circumspect…". A little further on, the ambassador adds: "The king is increasingly under the influence of the Illuminati…".

Ephraim was the most active instrument of the Girondins' alliance with Bischofswerder, adviser to the King of Prussia[269]. He was a skilful propagandist for Gensonné, Pétion and their

[267] *Foreign Affairs Archives*. Berlin, c. 212.

[268] *Idem.*

[269] Fr. Masson. *Le département des Affaires étrangères pendant la Révolution*, p. 102.

friends[270].

Arrested following the riot on the Champ de Mars, Ephraim was released two days later at the request of the Prussian ambassador. The curious thing is that the court in Vienna declares itself ready to support this request if necessary. The Marquis de Noailles observed that "this is one of the most unusual things of the moment"[271]. Moreover, after the arrest of Louis XVI at Varennes, the Austrian government, considering the French monarchy to be lost, began to draw closer to Prussia.

Moustiers wrote on 30 July: "Count de Goltz will be ordered to demand Ephraim's release and to formally disavow him as a revoked agent. I have been asked to inform you of this".

The research committee declares that it has carried out an exact verification of Ephraim's papers, "without however including the documents relating to his correspondence with His Majesty the King of Prussia, which were kept in a private portfolio".

So a foreign agent fomenting trouble in Paris is arrested, and his correspondence with the Prussian government is not even examined! This is quite extraordinary. Either he is covered by diplomatic immunity, and then how did he stay in prison from 28 to 30 July?[272] Or he is considered a spy, and so why is his political correspondence being respected—is it because it would compromise too many people?

Despite this weakness, the revolutionaries made a crime of Montmorin for having dared to have the Jew Ephraim arrested, and in the opinion of Fr. Masson, this was one of the main causes

---

[270] L. Kahn *The Jews of Paris*.

[271] *Archives of Foreign Affairs*, Vienna, v. 362, 6 August 1791.

[272] According to some authors, it's from the 18th to the 20th.

of the death of the unfortunate minister[273].

By giving Philippe Égalité's friends hope of a change of dynasty, Éphraïm had to laugh at their credulity. In reality, if he was preparing a candidacy, it was that of the Duke of Brunswick. The plan to place this prince on the throne of France was not just a joke on Carra's part, as some authors have appeared to believe. The beginnings of the negotiations can be found in the Foreign Affairs archives. The French group in the pay of Prussia was powerful enough to have made an official approach to Brunswick as early as January 1792. It was premature to offer him the crown, so he was offered the title of Generalissimo of the French armies. He would have restored order, granted all the reforms requested by the revolutionary party, and on the day Louis XVI was deposed, would have been ready to take his place. The minister Narbonne, without Louis XVI's knowledge, therefore sent the young Custine to the Duke of Brunswick, one of the leaders of Prussian Freemasonry. The king was indignant when he was informed of this, but since the return from Varennes he had been completely disarmed. Custine turned the conversation to "the importance of the role that could be played by a man of great character who, knowing how to maintain order within France and respect outside, would become the support of a revolution that would no longer present anything but advantages, the idol of the French, the benefactor of posterity…".

After obtaining the Duke's word of honour that what he was going to say to him would remain buried in eternal silence, "If the French nation," Custine continued, "were to declare through its representatives that in the crisis with which it is threatened, only one man is, by virtue of his past glory and the power of his genius and talents, capable of fulfilling these lofty destinies… and if this great man were you, Monseigneur, what would you

---

[273] Fr. MASSON. *Le département des Affaires étrangères pendant la Révolution,* p. 222.

say to us?

Deeply moved by these words, I saw that the Duke of Brunswick was also moved.

I recognise," he said, "the greatness of such an idea... But what man will be so presumptuous as to dare to believe he has the necessary strength? Then he added that he did not know enough about France... I gave him M. de Narbonne's letter. He was very moved by it, but he asked me some questions about the army and made some new objections about the difficulty of success: "You would think badly of me if I took a decision without thinking it through"[274].

The next day Brunswick replied that he saw too many difficulties with the party proposed to him: public opinion, which was too fickle in France, the incompatibility of his personal and family position with the offer made to him, and so on. Custine insisted without success: "This delicate tact, this deep knowledge of men and the French, all these nuances that you possess and which are necessary to lead them, prove to me that it is truly in France that you are called by nature to come and seek immortal glory".

Despite this pretender's lack of enthusiasm, his candidacy was not ruled out. In the week before the insurrection of 10 August, on the proposal of Manuel and Thuriot, the secret committee of the Jacobins approved the replacement of Louis XVI either by the Duke of York, the Duke of Brunswick or the Duke of Orléans[275]. As the throne became vacant after 10 August, the candidacy of the Prussian prince was officially put forward by Carra and his friends, no longer as Generalissimo, but as King of France. Carra, who had once been sentenced to prison

---

[274] *Foreign Affairs Archives.* Berlin, c. 213.

[275] G. Bord. *Autour du Temple,* I, p. 533.

for burglary, had a fairly good standing in the revolutionary world; six departments had competed for the honour of sending him to the Convention.

Sieyès and Talleyrand rallied to this proposal [276] ; but Robespierre and Billaut Varenne hastened to denounce to the Paris Commune the plot in favour of Brunswick "whom a powerful party wants to bring to the throne"[277]. They accused Condorcet of being an accomplice of Carra, as well as Vergniaud, Brissot, Lasource, Ducos and Guadet. As there were also two other candidates, the Duke of York and the Duke of Orléans, it was impossible to reach agreement.

The war had begun, and Brunswick had launched his famous manifesto, which has been portrayed as an insignificant blunder on the part of the émigrés. On the contrary, was it not a Machiavellian device on the part of Prussia to exasperate opinion in Paris and consummate the rupture between Louis XVI and the revolutionaries?

In the indictment against Brissot and Gensonné we read a very true sentence: "Nothing is so stupid as those who believe or would like others to believe that the Prussians want to destroy the Jacobins"[278].

Once hostilities had begun, Brunswick spared the French and never stopped negotiating with Jacobin emissaries. At the time of the battle of Valmy, he could have crushed Dumouriez's army, which was so outnumbered; he gave it time to receive reinforcements and supplies. After the battle, which was not very deadly, Dumouriez received formal orders not to disturb the

---

[276] LEBON. *England and emigration* (Introduction).

[277] AULARD. *Political history of the French Revolution.*

[278] *Archives nationales,* A. F. 11 45. *Report by Carra.*

Prussians' retreat[279].

The lack of enthusiasm aroused in France by Brunswick's candidacy seemed to have completely abandoned Carra's project. Moreover, this Prince was wary of the turbulence of his future subjects and the fate of Louis XVI had given him food for thought. Prince Louis of Prussia, who had always been sympathetic to France, was then considered. Sandoz, Prussia's minister in Paris, wrote in 1799: "Ste-Foy, Talleyrand's confidant, told me the following: The return of peace could depend on the restoration of a constitutional monarchy... The authorities and the healthy part of the nation would not decide for a Bourbon. They would rather vote for Prince Louis, son of Prince Ferdinand"[280].

Here is Albert Vandal's explanation of this plan to replace the Bourbon with a Prussian dynasty: "Some of the high revolutionaries imagined that by giving themselves to a pupil of the great Frederick, to a philosopher prince, the Revolution would achieve the most advantageous of ends...

Some were thinking of a protector and were thinking of making Brunswick reign, which would first be given a republican title"[281].

The unforeseen result of what Paul Bourget called "the defeat of the democratic illusion"![282]

It is impossible to trace the origin of a third Prussian candidate, that of Prince Henri, but there was certainly talk of

---

[279] The head of the Prussian forces and the Jacobins," said Oscar HAVARD, "agreed to offer France and Europe a mock battle".

[280] LEBON. *England and Emigration.* Preface, p. 27.

[281] *L'avènement de Bonaparte,* t. I, p. 118 et seq.

[282] P. BOURGET. *Testimony of experience.*

him before Prince Louis, since Empress Catherine of Russia wrote to Grimm on 11 June 1795: "There are people who claim that it is Prince Henri of Prussia whom the regicides intend to give as regent to Louis XVII when they re-establish him. If that is the case, I bet that within six months his Royal Highness will be guillotined"[283].

One wonders why a fine diplomat like Talleyrand was able to join this campaign of vulgar Jacobins, whom Ernest Renan described as "the ignorant and narrow-minded men who took the destiny of France into their own hands"[284]. Could he have believed in the solidity of a Prussian dynasty in our country? Or is the explanation to be found in Mirabeau's merciless portrait of Talleyrand: "A vile, greedy, base, scheming man. He needs mud and money. For money, he would sell his soul, and he would be right to do so, for he would trade his dung for gold"[285].

Presumably the campaign in favour of Brunswick was well paid to Carra and his friends; it would be difficult to explain it otherwise.

As for Sieyès, he received the portrait of the King of Prussia, estimated at the rather exaggerated figure of 100,000 ecus[286].

Mallet du Pan quoted Sieyès on these negotiations: "France needs a change of religion and dynasty"[287].

It should not be forgotten that the Strict Observance Reformed Templar Lodge in Germany, to which most of the French

---

[283] Ch. De Larivière. *Catherine II and the French Revolution*, p. 175.

[284] P. Lasserre. *Ernest Renan.*

[285] Barthou: *Mirabeau*, p. 157.

[286] Buchez and Roux. *Parliamentary History*, t. XXXVIII, p. 105.

[287] Lady Blennerhasset. *Mme de Staël and her time*, p. 105.

parliamentarians belonged, had Duke Ferdinand of Brunswick as its Grand Master. In addition, the Scottish rite took the lead in Berlin. This explains why the Prussian prince's candidacy was taken seriously.

One of Ephraim's fellow citizens also played an important role in the French Revolution, Baron Anacharsis Cloots, whom the suburbs insisted on calling Canard six. A Prussian Jew with more than a hundred thousand pounds in assets, Cloots was well known in the political world and would today be considered one of the 'Tout Paris des premières'.

He began by travelling to learn. In London he made friends with Burke, and in Holland with Castriotti, who called himself Prince of Albania. Suddenly he discovered that Castriotti was a simple brigand leader, condemned to death in absentia in his own country. Having almost been put in prison with his friend, Cloots stopped working on the Eastern question and came to Paris in 1784. He began to make revolutionary speeches. This was premature, as the upheaval had not yet been prepared, so police lieutenant Lenoir politely asked him to return to Prussia.

However, when the Estates General opened, Anacharsis Cloots, like all foreigners, resettled in Paris. A militant Freemason, he was one of the promoters of the anti-Catholic movement. He could not speak of a priest without immediately going into a rage[288]. Treated by Marat and Camille Desmoulins as a Berlin snitch[289], he nevertheless quickly acquired great influence thanks to his hundred thousand pounds of income. Cloots took an active part in the preparations for 10 August, but as a wise man he was careful not to expose himself to blows. His eulogist, Avenel, recounts that he "threw his two sans-culotte servants into the insurrectionary flood. As for himself, he ran to

---

[288] Louis BLANC. *La Révolution Française,* t. IX, p. 474.

[289] Avenel. *Anacharsis Cloots*, Ch. I.

the Assembly to be only two steps away from the party, perhaps even to breathe in the smell of gunpowder and receive the baptism of fire in case a stray cannonball pierced the vault of the hall".

Having inhaled the smell of gunpowder from afar, he left the Assembly at the same time as Louis XVI and stood guard in the courtyard of the Manège to prevent the king from being freed.

The following night, Cloots returned to the Assembly, surrounded by Prussian federates, including Colonel Guerresheim, and delivered a patriotic speech which was ordered to be sent to the 83 departments and the army.

With such a fine record of service, it comes as no surprise that Cloots was appointed deputy for the departments of Oise and Saône-et-Loire.

He had already been put in charge of the diplomatic and war committees[290]. He became president of the Jacobin Club at the very moment when the decree against foreigners had just been published. He had previously written to Dumouriez: "Crush the enemies outside while I crush the enemies inside"[291].

Dining at Roland's at the time of the September massacres, he approved of "popular vengeance"[292]. Mme Roland observed that he bored more than one listener with his speeches, but she did not mention any protests.

It is difficult to say whether Anacharsis Cloots was a direct agent of the Prussian government, or merely a collaborator of the occult syndicate that directed our Revolution. He claimed to be

[290] *Archives nationales*, A. D. XVIII, 17.

[291] *Id.* at F. 7, 4649.

[292] De la Gorce: *Histoire religieuse de la Révolution.*

estranged from his country, but he was in correspondence with the Duke of Brunswick[293].

We don't know whether he was mad or just posing for originality.

One of the organisers of the festival of the goddess Reason at Notre-Dame, he went one night with Pereyra to wake Bishop Gobel in order to persuade him to abjure. Calling himself "the orator of the human race", Cloots one day disguised vagabonds as Turks, Indians, Persians, etc., and brought them to the Convention to demand a universal republic. We all know the eloquent conclusion of his famous speech: "My heart is French and my soul is a sans-culotte".

Cloots had found a way of stopping the invasion of 1792: he proposed that the French army, confronted by the Prussians and Austrians, should "advance towards them with a dance step expressing friendship"[294]. Unfortunately, the generals opposed this attempt.

Cloots, Paine and Robert, all three foreigners, were the first to speak of a republic, when no Frenchman had even thought of it. As early as 21 April 1792, the orator of humankind stood before the Assembly and extolled this form of government.

Anacharsis Cloots worked actively to have Louis XVI sentenced to death. After 21 January, he wrote to a friend: "I would like to wash my hands, baptised in the blood of Louis XVI, in the blood of the last tyrant"[295].

Unfortunately, during the Terror, the popularity of Anacharsis

---

[293] *Archives nationales*, F. 7, 4438.

[294] T. De WYZEWA: *Excentriques et aventuriers*, p. 165.

[295] Richter: *Cloots*. This work, published in Berlin, has not yet been translated.

Cloots was demolished by Robespierre who was suspicious, he said, of a sans-culotte with a hundred thousand pounds of income. Having let slip these words: "my disciple Robespierre forgets the lessons of his teacher", he attracted the following apostrophe: "Cloots you spend your life with the agents and the spies of the foreign powers." Already Brissot, after having been his friend, had written in the *Patriote Français:* A lot of malice, a variable course, an unknown goal, here is Cloots[296].

He once dared to show his independence from Freemasonry by opposing the proposal to reserve all public offices for Freemasons only[297].

Cloots claims to have fought on the diplomatic committee "against the English faction that predominated there". Nevertheless, he was arrested as an accomplice of Pitt, along with Hébert, Ronsin, Chabot, Fabre—d'Églantine, Momoro, Chaumette and Gobel[298]. They were planning, it was claimed, to give dictatorship to the mayor of Paris, Pache.

The seals were placed at Cloots's, the suspect papers were put aside; the minutes list his entire wardrobe: twelve pairs of slippers, a beard plate, seven suit buttons, a pair of sleeve buttons, etc.[299] . Not a word about his correspondence with Prussia and England. That would be interesting!

Cloots was condemned and guillotined.

A few other Prussians played a more discreet role in the revolutionary period. Pastor Bitaubé, born in Kœnigsberg, was a

---

[296] *Archives nationales*, A. D. XVIII I 17.

[297] F. Caussy: *Choderlos de Laclos*, p. 158.

[298] L. Madelin: *The French Revolution.*

[299] *Archives nationales*, F. 7, 2507, and F. 7, 4649.

talented writer. His translation *of Homer,* a number of poems and various works brought him to the Berlin Academy. Méhul set his *Joseph* poem to music.

One wonders why Bitaubé found himself in Paris at the start of the Revolution, a member of the Jacobin club, living in the milieu of Cerutti and Ximénes, often treating Robespierre to dinner.

General Thiébault used to sit at his table on Thursday evenings with Chamfort and Hélène Williams, an Englishwoman who was an enthusiast of the Revolution.

While the French literati were proscribed[300], it was proposed to the Convention to vote a pension for Bitaubé. Kéralio wrote to him: "Brissot, Carra and all your friends in the Convention must raise their voices in support of this act of justice"[301].

Bitaubé was arrested during the Terror and released on 9 Thermidor. Little is known about his political role, but he was undoubtedly to collaborate with his Jacobin friends. A mysterious letter sent from London via Frankfurt on 24 May 1793 seems to relate to revolutionary activities and expresses the hope that Bitaubé will understand abbreviations. Other documents concerning him have disappeared from the archives.

In year VI, Bitaubé became President of the Institut.

---

[300] Louis Blanc credited the. Révolution the glory of having founded the Institut, it is worth recalling the creation of five academies by Louis XIV: the Académie Française, the Académie des inscriptions et belles-lettres, the Académie des sciences, the Académie de peinture et de sculpture, and the Académie d'architecture. They were all abolished by the law of 8 August 1793, which Michelet and L. Blanc ignore. Almost all the academicians were proscribed. See BIRÉ: *Légendes révolutionnaires.*

[301] *Archives nationales,* F. 7, 4601.

The Baroness d'Aelders, the daughter of a Groningen innkeeper, was a secret agent of the Prussian government. In the last years of the reign of Louis XVI, she founded a club of revolutionary women in Paris, "*les amies de la vérité*". Protected by Condorcet, Mme d'Aelders was in league with Basire, the deputy from Dijon. This Jacobin was quite humane: he protested against the September massacres and delayed the trial of the Girondins after having accused them. As "he knew how to refuse nothing to women"[302], it is probable that it was Mme d'Aelders who pushed him to attack the king, the court, Lafayette, etc., but it was not Mme d'Aelders who pushed him to attack the king.

Arrested after the Champ de Mars riot, Mme d'Aelders was soon released, thanks to high-level influence. She was imprisoned again on 5 Messidor, Year II, and seals were placed on the mezzanine floor she lived in at 11, rué Favart. The Committee of General Safety gave the order to extract suspicious correspondence from her papers; the commissioners stated that they had put the said papers "in an armchair cover that we have cracked open, and have put the seal of our committee on both ends and have had the whole thing taken to our committee"[303].

Unfortunately, these papers have disappeared, as have all those of foreign agents.

G. Forster, the son of a pastor from Danzig, accompanied Cook around the world, was in turn an alchemist, professor at the University of Vilna and librarian at the University of Mainz. A Rosicrucian Freemason, a member of the Jacobin club in Mainz after the conquest of that city, and a passionate admirer of the French Revolution, Forster was in regular correspondence with Lebrun-Tondu and some of our politicians. On 5 June 1792, he announced the forthcoming overthrow of royalty. In 1793, he

---

[302] *Great encyclopaedia.* Article by M. AULARD on Basire.

[303] *Archives nationales*, F. 7, 4659.

settled in Paris, spoke at the Convention, dined with Merlin de Thionville, Théroigne de Méricour, Lecouteulx de Canteleu, Rewbell, Lecointre, etc., and was a great admirer of the French Revolution.

He was appointed Commissioner of the Executive Council in June 1793, and the Ministry of Foreign Affairs entrusted him with two missions, to Flanders and Franche-Comté[304].

A friend of Thomas Paine and Miss Williams, he became a counter-revolutionary after the Terror, like his compatriot Adam Lux, who, after joining the Jacobin movement, defended Charlotte Corday and was sentenced to death for it.

Schlabrendorf, born in Silesia, was so absorbed by the Revolution that for several years he forgot to give notice of the house he had rented in London before moving to Paris. A very wealthy man, during the revolutionary period he lived in a modest flat where he entertained a large number of friends.

He continued to conspire under the Consulate without being much talked about.

Doctor J. Eric-Bolmann (Hanoverian) settled in Paris with an uncle, an English subject. He says that he was pushed against his will, by pikes, into the middle of the insurrection of 10 August. Disgusted with Paris, he left, saving Narbonne with an English passport, at the request of Mme de Staël[305].

Others include Trenck, who sacrificed his fortune for "the satisfaction of living in the land of liberty"[306], the tailor Nestch, who was part of a plot to assassinate Lafayette, Rabbi Hourwitz,

---

[304] Chuquet: *Études d'Histoire*, 1ère series, p. 234.

[305] LADY BLENNERHASSET: Mme *de Staël et son temps,* vol. II, p. 158 ff.

[306] Avenel: *Anarchasis Cloots*, p. 182 ff.

a friend of Fauchet and Clavière, Aelsner, Campe, Huber, Ancillon, Archenholz, Goy and Eschim Portaek, a member of the Jacobin Club.

To sum up, Prussia's role was particularly important at the beginning of the Revolution. After the overthrow of the French monarchy, the Berlin cabinet handed over to the English government.

It seems that these two powers combined their efforts against Louis XVI. At the time of the change of ministry on 12 July 1789, the English ambassador to France, having immediately sent a letter to his government, hurried to send another to the King of Prussia. As soon as this letter arrived, "an Extraordinary Committee was convened; Prince Henri was not called... The Court would like the troubles in France to be more serious and to last forever"[307].

The reason for Prince Henry of Prussia's exclusion was his sympathy for France, which was pointed out by all those who came into contact with him.

When there was talk of putting the Duke of Brunswick on the throne of France, the British government did not oppose it; it did not believe in the success of the Duke of York's candidacy. Brunswick, brother-in-law of the King of England, was under his influence. As early as 1876, Mercy Argenteau pointed out to Kaunitz the subsidies paid to Brunswick by the London cabinet, and in 1789, Moustiers stated that the King of Prussia's entourage had been sold out to England.

But our statesmen have never taken the secret dealings of foreign governments in Paris seriously. We have an example of this that is too recent to be forgotten: we know how sceptically

---

[307] *Foreign Affairs Archives.* Correspondence from Berlin, July, 1789.

M. Léon Daudet's volume "L'Avant-Guerre" was received in 1914. It seems that the French Revolution was prepared with the same skill as the recent invasion of the barbarians from across the Rhine.

CHAPTER IX

ENGLISH AGENTS

O f the foreigners who invaded France in 1789 and worked on the Revolution, the English were by far the most numerous; but, with a few exceptions, they disguised themselves more skilfully than the others.

Here are the main ones:

Among the cosmopolitan revolutionaries was a rather sympathetic character, a philosopher who was charitable and devoted to his friends, Thomas Paine (or Payne), who had the courage to speak out at the Convention against the death of Louis XVI.

A clerk in the English customs service, Paine had been dismissed from his post; he set himself up as a tobacco merchant, then a corset maker, then a grocer. Not seeing his fortune coming, he enlisted in America and was appointed aide-de-camp to General Greene. Charged with negotiating a loan in Paris, he received substantial bonuses from the American government. He then increased his fortune by building bridges. Suddenly he discovered his literary vocation and began writing pamphlets.

Arriving in Paris in 1787, Paine was due to leave the following year, but, he says, "the desire to contribute with all my power to the French Revolution caused me to postpone my return... The plan I proposed for the great work is still in Barère's hands[308]". So in 1788, Paine knew that the Revolution was about to break out.

He was the author of the Declaration of the Rights of Man, as well as of the address attributed to Colonel du Châtelet concluding that the monarchy should be abolished. This declaration, of which our democrats are so proud, is therefore the work of England.

Together with Pétion, Lafayette and Buzot, Paine founded a club which met at Condorcet's house and worked on the revolutionary movement.

In July 1791, Paine returned to London because Lafayette, not having to employ him in Paris, asked him to carry the key to the Bastille to Franklin[309]. But he was poorly received by his fellow citizens because of his republican views, and returned to settle permanently in Paris. A triumphal entry had been prepared for him when he disembarked at Calais. The soldiers formed a hedge as he passed; the officers embraced him and led him to the Hôtel de Ville, where he was again embraced by the Municipality.

Paine was a member of the committee responsible for preparing the new constitution. Appointed member of the Convention by three departments, Oise, Puy-de-Dôme and Pas-de-Calais, he inspired Brissot's articles. Mme Roland pointed out to Bancal the formation of a Republican Society led by Paine. It was he," she wrote in 1791, "who provided the material for the prospectus displayed this morning on all sides"[310].

One of his friends, Wilkes, having been arrested in Paris and condemned, had an urgent and mysterious reason for returning to

---

[308] *Archives nationales*, F. 7, 2775.

[309] Letter from Gower to Grenville.

[310] Correspondence from Mme Roland.

England for a few days; Paine obtained a safe-conduct for him, undertaking to take Wilkes' place in prison. He returned and was lucky enough to escape the guillotine.

Mme Roland compared Paine's face to a blackberry sprinkled with flour. As he did not know French, his friends read his speeches to the Convention while Paine made the gestures. It can be seen that the sessions of the terrible assembly were not lacking in a certain gaiety.

Paine lived in a veritable den of English conspiracy, the White Hotel on the Passage des Petit-Pères. There were Stone, Smyth, E. Fitz-Gerald, Yorke, Captain Monro and others. They drank so dry that Paine became an alcoholic.

After the massacres, which he disapproved of, he advised putting Louis XVI on trial; convinced that the king was going to be assassinated, he thought he could save him in this way. He wanted the overthrow of the French Monarchy, but cruelty was repugnant to him. Speaking in defence of the sovereign at the Convention, Thomas Paine explained that we should show compassion, because we could only see in this monarch "an ill-bred man like all his fellows".

It is likely that Louis XVI's poor education prevented him from thanking his defender.

After opposing the death penalty, Paine proposed sending the royal family to America.

From then on Robespierre declared him a suspect. Paine had also made an enemy of Marat by denouncing his plans for a dictatorship to the Jacobin Club. He therefore did not escape proscription. Paine initially hid under the protection of Samson, the executor of the High Works, but this ingenious hiding place was eventually discovered. The policemen in charge of arresting him say that the search had upset their stomachs, so they began by having lunch; then, having discovered the inventor of the Declaration of the Rights of Man, "we were unable," they said, "to make ourselves heard by him, being American; for which reason we begged the principal tenant of the said house to kindly serve as our interpreter... Not wishing to leave any doubt as to our conduct, we requested that all the cupboards be opened"[311].

But, after a scrupulous examination, Paine's papers did not appear to contain anything suspicious; which did not prevent him from being put in the Luxembourg prison. He owed his life to a lucky chance, unless that chance had been aided by the Anglo-Prussian Syndicate—for it should be noted that foreigners always got out of prison more easily than Frenchmen. Every day, the gaoler at the Luxembourg marked with chalk the cells of the prisoners who were to be executed the next day. Paine was included in a list of 160 condemned prisoners, but the door of his cell was open because he had a fever; the white cross was marked on the inside of the door. When the cell was closed in the evening, the cross was no longer visible from the outside[312]. The next morning, only 159 prisoners were counted instead of 160. Paine was therefore undoubtedly replaced at random by the first person who came along.

Perhaps not suspecting the danger from which he had escaped, the prisoner wrote in all directions to protest against his detention. Robespierre," he told the Convention, "was my inveterate enemy, as he was of all men of virtue and humanity. Finally, after eight months, Paine was released thanks to several interventions (13 Brumaire, year III).

After this alert he seems to have played a more discreet role. He stopped going to the Convention, but according to Bourdon, "he intrigued with a former foreign agent, Louis Otto". There is

---

[311] *Archives nationales*, F. 7, 2775.

[312] Fortiolis: *Un Anglais membre de la Convention*, Revue hebdomadaire, 1914.

no trace of his subsequent dealings with the British government.

Under the Directoire, Paine did not make a name for himself. In 1802, he left for America, kidnapping the wife of a journalist friend of his. He died an alcoholic in 1809.

His fellow citizen W. A. Miles, Pitt's agent, exerted a certain influence on our ministers, as this letter from Lebrun-Tondu proves: "I am short eighteen louis for the discharge of a bill of exchange. Could you not add this new benefit to all the gratitude I owe you?

The Reverend Ch. Miles, in publishing his grandfather's correspondence, was astonished at the disappearance of W. A. Miles's letters to Pitt from 1790 to 1793. "They must have been the most interesting," he observed. Was it not precisely because they were too interesting that the English government did not want to leave them in the hands of his agent's heirs?

Miles says he was secretly sent to Paris for the same reason as his friend Hugh Elliot.

Holland Rose, in Pitt's story, explains that their mission was "to influence the French democrats".

At the time when Pétion introduced Miles to the Jacobin Club, he was living at 113, Faubourg Saint-Honoré; he was in frequent contact with Barnave, Mirabeau, Lafayette, Frochot, and so on. Unfortunately, Miles' letters, which contain nothing incriminating, are the only ones to have been published. In September 1790 he announced to Pitt that the monarchy would soon be abolished in France. At that time, there was not a single member of parliament who was not a monarchist and not a single Frenchman who called himself a republican.

Miles' correspondence proves that he has a poor idea of his friends the Jacobins: "Nothing good can be expected from such an assembly of thieves, murderers, etc." (5 January 1791). "If you attribute the Revolution to a virtuous sentiment or a courageous effort, you are mistaken" (18 March 1791). Miles complained at this time that his correspondence was intercepted, so his letters became more banal[313].

In the XIXᵉ century, several of Miles' great-grandsons became French; the best known is Ambassador Waddington.

Hugh Elliot, who worked with Miles, was Lord Auckland's brother-in-law. A former pupil of Mirabeau's at the Choquart boarding school, he was given special responsibility for influencing the famous orator in favour of England[314].

Hugh Elliot wrote to Pitt on 26 October 1790: "I cannot confide to paper the account of my secret conversations with various political personages. But I have every reason to believe that, more than anyone else, I am master of events"[315].

There are hints that Mirabeau and others did not refuse English money, but Holland Rose adds: "Our two envoys were discreet enough to give few details in their letters.

Dracke, an English spy, attended the secret meetings of the Comité de Salut Public and gave an accurate account of them to Lord Grenville. On 2 September 1792, he told him that that evening 2,250 suspects had been designated for arrest. The death of Marie-Antoinette and the Brissotins had been decided, and 500,000 francs had been given to Pache to foment a riot in the

---

[313] Miles acted as an intermediary between Danton and the English Ministry, particularly during the trial of Louis XVI.

[314] Pallain: *Talleyrand's Mission to London*, p. 234.

[315] Hollland Rose: *William Pitt*, p. 581. This work has not yet been translated into French.

first days of September[316].

Mr Aulard takes the view that Dracke only passed on information concerning foreign policy. But if the secrets of our diplomacy were entrusted to him, why should internal affairs have been concealed from him? Billaud Varennes and Hérault de Séchelles accused each other of this treason. They may both have been right, for Hérault de Séchelles was taking diplomatic files to communicate them to the son of the Austrian minister Kaunitz; and Billaud Varennes was secretly sending reports of what was happening in government circles to Venice and Spain. Their names were again mentioned during the capture of Toulon; correspondence was seized from a traitor who could only be one of the members of the Committee of Public Safety[317].

Dracke does not appear to have been troubled in his profession throughout the revolutionary period; he was only prosecuted at the time of Georges Cadoudal's plot, as he was one of his auxiliaries.

The Girondins met on Sunday evenings in the salon of Hélène Williams, a friend of Mme Roland. She was a great influence on Bancal, Brissot, Achille du Châtelet, Miranda, Lasource, Sillery, Girey-Dupré and Rabaut Saint-Etienne. Mme Roland wanted to marry her to Bancal, but the young Englishwoman preferred her fellow citizen Stone, who followed her everywhere. We have not been able to find out whether they pushed the revolutionary spirit as far as a free union, or whether Hélène Williams only allowed Stone a platonic love. She never bore his name; it has been wondered whether they were secretly married. But a police report to the Revolutionary Committee states that Stone's wife has a

---

[316] *Historical manuscripts commission* (Appendix I). *The manuscripts of J. B. Fortescue*, vol. II, p. 457.

[317] Mathiez: *Histoire secrète du Comité de Salut public*.

fortune of £60,000 (over 1,500,000 francs)[318]. It is therefore likely that Stone left his wife to follow Helene Williams, but did not divorce her.

Arrested in October 1793, then released, Hélène Williams took refuge in Switzerland until 9 Thermidor. Back in Paris with Stone, she undoubtedly continued her political activities, as she was arrested again in 1802, following a police search of her papers.

Stone, one of the victors of the Bastille, was very close to Brissot, Pétion and M. and Mme de Genlis. When she went abroad, she entrusted her papers to Stone, who gave them to Hélène Williams. On learning that her home was to be searched, the young Englishwoman burnt Madame de Genlis's papers.

To justify his presence in Paris, Stone set up a printing works. When suspected of conspiracy, he claimed to be completely absorbed in his business. He managed to get himself appointed president of the "Friends of Human Rights" club, and to acquire a certain influence.

Lord Stanhope wrote to Grenville: "Mr Stone is an Englishman who knows the ministers and the leading men in France well... He will be able to convince you of their good intentions.

Stone was having dinner parties with Milnes and R. Smith, Pitt's agents. At one of their orgies, an Englishman, after copious libations, punched Paine in the face and then fled in horror at his crime. But the next day they were reconciled[319].

Stone testified on Miranda's behalf. Arrested twice and

---

[318] *Archives nationales*, F. 7, 4778.

[319] *Archives nationales*, F. 7, 4778.

released, he took refuge in Switzerland where he met up with Hélène Williams. He returned with her after 9 Thermidor.

William Stone, brother of the former, prosecuted for conspiracy in England, then acquitted, had settled in Villeneuve-Saint-Georges in 1789, with a fellow countryman, Parker. The Stone brothers claim to have paid 12,000 francs to escape Sillery, which Mme de Genlis refused to reimburse.

Stone's correspondence arrived from England under cover of Auguste Rose. He took part in the main riots: in the Algiers volume on the role of the English in the French Revolution[320], Rose is listed as one of the Convention's ten "ushers" (one of the ten ushers, etc.). On 9 Thermidor, he was in charge of leading Robespierre and his supporters to the Committee of Public Safety. Rose was arrested by order of the Commune; he shoved his guards and escaped. He then tried to go unnoticed.

David Williams, who was not related to Hélène Williams, worked with Roland and Brissot, who translated his work on liberty. Naturalised as a Frenchman, he declared in November 1792 that he was "surrendering to the wishes of his new homeland and will contribute to the edifice of happiness and prosperity that the Convention must erect"[321]. However, William was only half as fond of his revolutionary friends as he was of the members of the Convention: "Carelessness, recklessness and filth do not make a legislator commendable.

Mme Roland's letters prove that the Girondins' campaign for press freedom was dictated by Williams and the English journalist R. Pigott.

The Société des Amis des Noirs had as its apparent aim the

---

[320] *Englishmen in the French revolution* (Algiers).

[321] *Foreign Office Archives*, London, v. 583.

emancipation of Negroes, and as its hidden object the Universal Republic. One of its main founders was Robert Pigott, an English Quaker and friend of Roland and Lanthenas. Alongside him were Clarkson, Mirabeau's collaborator, and the very French names of Wilberforce, Paine, Williams, Daer, son of the Earl of Selkirk, Sharp and Grenville[322]. Bolstered by England, the Société des Amis des Noirs published *the Observateur, a* newspaper edited by Faydel, a friend of Laclos[323]. Pigott invented the red bonnet. On 10 February 1790, the National Assembly voted to print one of his speeches.

Two other Pigotts also worked during the Revolution: one was a Shropshire magistrate; the other, a pamphleteer, John Pigott, sometimes known as Jean Picotte, was arrested in 1793 and released the following year.

Why did Benjamin Vaughan live in Passy under the name of Jean Martin? Why did he frequently visit Robespierre in secret?[324] The son of a wealthy English merchant, he had married Miss Manning, a member of the Cardinal's family, so he must have had a fairly good situation in London, where he claimed to be in trouble because of his political opinions. After making a series of speeches in Nantes, Vaughan joined the Société des *Amis de la Révolution* in 1791. Apart from Robespierre, only four or five people knew Vaughan's identity (Bishop Grégoire, Hamilton Rowan, etc.). Arrested in 1794, the false Jean Martin was nearly put to death as an agent of Pitt. But after a month in detention, he obtained a passport for Switzerland from the Comité de Salut Public.

---

[322] They include the banker Kornmann, a member of the Commune and famous for his marital misfortunes.

[323] DARD: *Choderlos de Laclos.*

[324] M. Mathiez (*Annales révolutionnaires of February 1917*) denies Vaughan's intimacy with Robespierre; but it is affirmed by Barère.

The poet Barlow was mainly involved in revolutionary propaganda in Savoy, while Alfieri sang of the storming of the Bastille and Klopstock glorified the French Revolution.

During the winter of 1792, an English ship belonging to Martin Milleth landed in the port of Boulogne. The next day, the captain and all the crew disappeared[325]. The police searched but found nothing. No one knew what had become of them, except Pitt, who had obviously given them each their own job.

Watt, son of the famous inventor, and his friend the druggist Th. Cooper, were the organisers of a demonstration in honour of the revolted soldiers of Châteauvieux. Friends of Marat, they approved 10 August, donated 1,300 francs for the families of patriots wounded during the insurrection, but took the liberty of criticising the massacres. Robespierre takes advantage of this to denounce them as agents of Pitt. Watt escapes to Italy and Cooper to America.

J. Oswald, pamphleteer and poet, friend of Brissot, was one of the founders of the *Chronique du mois.* In March 1792, he put up placards in the Faubourg Saint-Antoine demanding the distribution of pikes to all citizens and the abolition of the standing armies.

Tasked with organising a regiment of federates, Oswald was sent to the Vendée and killed in the first battle, probably by his own troops, because he had made himself intolerable and his soldiers hated him.

La Luzerne, ambassador in London, mentions a Pitt agent in Paris in the entourage of the Duke of Orléans: a man called Forth, who frequently travelled between France and England[326]. Three

---

[325] *Archives nationales*, D. XXIX.

[326] *Foreign Office Archives*, London, v. 588.

members of the Paris Commune corresponded with Choderlos de Laclos, Philippe Égalité's confidant, through Forth. Forth faithfully reported to Pitt on the actions of the Duke of Orléans. His collaborators were Smith, Clarke and Shee.

Mathews, a secret agent for the British government, changes his name when he comes under suspicion in Paris. He corresponded frequently with our politicians. One day, the Comité de salut public paid fifteen thousand livres owed by Mathews to his hotelier[327]. Given the state of French finances, this generosity seems quite extraordinary!

On 7 September 1793, Mathews asked Danton for a security passport because he was worried. He was right, for his arrest had been decided the day before. Otto had run to warn him, but had missed him. Mathews was therefore arrested and the police sealed an important correspondence with Danton, Hérault de Séchelles and others. A letter dated 19 September reminds the minister: "You promised me that I would be released immediately". We do not know whether the minister kept his promise.

It was largely Mathews' influence that brought the German Reinhardt into our Foreign Office, where he became a skilled diplomat.

The bankers Boyd and Kerr had made the acquaintance of the revolutionary Genevois when the refugees of 1782 received a million from the English government. They moved to Paris in 1789, first to rue d'Amboise and then to rue de Grammont, where they became involved in politics and had business dealings with Philippe Égalité. They acted as intermediaries to pay some of the leaders of the French Revolution; they were members of the Club

---

[327] *Archives des Affaires étrangères*, France, c. 1408.

de Valois.

The seals having been placed on the bank in the rue de Grammont, Boyd had to pay 200,000 pounds to have them removed; then he judged it prudent to sell up and take refuge in England. Pitt then entrusted him with several secret missions.

After the death of Louis XVI, Boyd and Kerr joined Jean de Batz's plot, and for this reason were condemned on 29 Prairial, year II. The reports of the Comité de Salut Public stated that Boyd and Kerr were direct agents of Pitt[328].

Frey and Chabot tried to have their papers unsealed. Robespierre opposed them, but Batz succeeded through Luillier's mediation, and had everything connected with his plots removed. Boyd was closely related to the member of the English Parliament who bore his name.

We have already pointed out that the Commune's Revolutionary Committee was almost entirely made up of foreigners: the Swiss Pache, the Italians Pio and Dufourny, the Spaniard Guzman, the Englishman Arthur[329], etc. J.-J. Arthur is mentioned in Robespierre's diaries among the fairly skilful patriots. J.-J. Arthur is mentioned in Robespierre's notebooks among the fairly skilful patriots. He must have been quite wealthy, as he owned the house opposite the Pavillon de Hanovre, as evidenced by a lawsuit he brought against the Richelieu family.

J.-J Arthur had links with Pache, Marat, and the Proly gang, Gusman, Frey, etc. President of the Section des Piques, he prepared the riot on the Champ de Mars. A member of the

---

[328] *Archives nationales*, W. 389, n° 904.

[329] Arthur was born in Paris to an English father (V. Mathiez, *La Révolution et les étrangers)*.

Central Committee of the Paris Commune, he often spoke at the Jacobin Club; he testified against Danton and Clavière, at Robespierre's request; he was a member of the Committee appointed to support the Incorruptible against the Convention. It is well known that Robespierre never ceased to denounce the *foreign faction.* Yet his Committee included five foreigners out of eight members, and this detail cast doubt on Robespierre's independence.

Arthur was guillotined on 12 Thermidor.

Dobsent (or Dobsen), president of the Revolutionary Court, was also of English origin. It was he who had organised the insurrection of 31 May. A friend of Lazowski and Desfieux, Dobsent frequented the gang of Proly and Pereyra. The fall of the Girondins was prepared at their meetings at the Café Corazza[330]. Arrested first with the Hébertistes, and again after the riot of 1er April 1795, Dobsent took part in the Jacobin activities of 1799 and always managed to escape. He was appointed judge under the Empire, although his record reads: "Mediocre talents, below the level of the duties he would have to perform, etc."[331].

Earl Charles Stanhope, a member of the English House of Peers, was Pitt's brother-in-law by his first marriage and Grenville's son-in-law by his second. After spending his youth in Geneva, where he met the Swiss revolutionaries, Stanhope became one of the leaders of English Masonry. In this capacity he was to take an interest in the French Revolution, and indeed he played an important role in the Lodge of United Friends, which prepared the fall of the Monarchy[332].

---

[330] A. Schmidt: *Paris pendant la Révolution, d'après les rapports de la police secrète,* p. 149 ff.

[331] *Archives nationales,* F. 7, 6504.

[332] A grandfather had played a major role in Law's bankruptcy.

Stanhope had frequent meetings with Philippe Égalité and undoubtedly lulled him with the hope of a change of dynasty. Once the throne had been overthrown, Stanhope lost interest in France and turned his attention back to the sciences. He invented addition and subtraction machines and left a volume on electricity.

Another English scientist was involved in the 1789 plot: Priestley, born in Yorkshire, was a professor of physics and chemistry; after a wealthy marriage, he became a clergyman in Birmingham.

On 26 August 1792, on the basis of a report by Guadet, a decree granted French citizenship to a number of foreigners for services rendered to the revolutionary cause, including Priestley, Paine, J. Bentham, Wilberforce, Th. Clarkson, Mackintosch, David Williams and Madison.

Appointed a member of the Convention by two departments, Priestley did not wish to take his seat; but his influence was considerable, since Burges wrote to Lord Auckland: "Priestley is regarded as the principal adviser to the Ministry. His advice is taken on all occasions"[333].

Having wanted to celebrate 14 July with his friends in Birmingham, he was unpleasantly surprised to see his house ransacked by a mob outraged by his revolutionary views. He therefore decided it would be wiser to leave England for good, and after another stay in France, Priestley settled in America.

A Presbyterian, Priestley embraced the religion of Arminius, then became an Arian, then a Socinian; he always remained the enemy of Catholicism.

---

[333] Papers of Lord Auckland, 4 September 1792.

Priestley left many learned works. He is credited with the discovery of nitrogen[334].

Alongside these illustrious men was a veritable army of English conspirators.

Thomas Christie, from a family of academics, became a close friend of Danton and Cloots.

Paul Waiworth is employed directly by the King of England[335].

Sheare, one of Théroigne de Méricour's lovers, was, like his brother, a close friend of Roland and Brissot.

S. Perry, a journalist, dined with Danton, Condorcet, Brissot and Santerre; he testified in favour of Marat.

Pastor Goodwin abandoned his career to take up the cause of the Revolution. Associated with Paine, he left works that are widely read in England; M. H. Roussin has just devoted a volume to him. Goodwin lived more in London than in Paris, while his wife lived more in Paris than in London; he had married Mary Wollstonecraft, qualified as a professor in various documents.

Mrs Wollstonecraft-Goodwin violently attacked Marie-Antoinette, even after her death; she was so exalted in her revolutionary ideas that Horace Walpole called her a "hyena in petticoats". One of her friends, Hamilton Rowan, an Irish agitator and friend of Robespierre, left Paris immediately after the arrest of the Incorruptible.

Lord Palmerston ostensibly frequented revolutionary circles,

---

[334] In praise of Priestley at the Institut, delivered by Cuvier.

[335] *Foreign Office archives*, London, v. 577.

while Lord Camelsford, a relative of Pitt and Grenville, concealed himself with a passport under a false name.

The adventurer Newton is appointed colonel of the first division of the National Guard.

Kerly, an agent for the Herries bank and a regular member of the Jacobin Club, is denounced as a spy.

Quintin Cranfurd conspired with Fersen to save the Queen; it is not known whether he began, like his compatriots, by conspiring against the Monarchy.

The Earl of Devonshire is commander of the Récollets district.

Wendling (or Wendlen) was a member of the Insurrectionary Committee on 31 May[336].

Among the regulars at Mme de Condorcet's salon were Lord Stormon, Lord Stanhope, Lord Dear, Jefferson, Bache, Franklin, etc., not to mention Anacharsis Cloots, who was in love with the lady of the house[337].

According to Louis Blanc, the Scotsman Swinton, who with Brissot founded the newspaper Le *Patriote Français,* had the bizarre profession of "speculator in debauchery"[338].

An English merchant, Marshall, founded the revolutionary newspaper *l'Union* in 1789. Blackwood, arrested during the

---

[336] *Actes de la Commune*, t. VII, p. 492.

[337] Michelet: *Women of the Revolution.* A. Guillois: *The Marquise of Condorcet.* A. Guillois: *The salon of Mme Helvétius.*

[338] Louis Blanc: *History of the French Revolution.*

Terror as a foreign agent, was saved by Chabot; it is suspected that his guineas had not been without influence on Chabot's benevolence[339].

H.-R. Yorke boasted that at the age of twenty-two he had taken part in the three revolutions in America, Holland and France[340]. But he must have been getting younger, because although he was twenty-two in 1789, he was only eight when he was sentenced to prison in 1775, and twelve when he married his jailer's daughter in 1779. Related to Paine, he was a member of the Friends of the Rights of Man club, attended sessions of the Convention and associated with leading Jacobins. H. Yorke's real name was Readhead. Denounced to the Convention at the end of 1793 as a foreign agent, he fled to Switzerland. He is known to have written a work entitled *Lettres de France*, which is a picture of French life and customs under the Consulate[341].

Holcroft worked as a groom, shoemaker, schoolmaster, journalist, actor and playwright before entering politics after the death of his three wives. He translated Mirabeau's works into English. Holcroft was a friend of Danton and related to his family[342].

Smith is a judge at the Finistère Revolutionary Court; O'Brien is a judge in Saint-Malo. The spy Ducket is Léonard Bourdon's secretary.

Rutlidge (or Rutledge) belonged to an excellent Irish family. During the reign of Louis XV, he came to Paris to amuse himself, then began his literary career with a tragedy in French. Under

---

[339] Vte de Bonald: *F. Chabot*, p. 138.

[340] L. Fortiolis: *An English member of the Convention.*

[341] T. de Wyzewa: *Eccentrics and adventurers.*

[342] His daughter married Mergès, nephew of Danton.

Louis XVI, he wrote for the "Quinzaine Anglaise" and had a number of comedies performed, but they were not very successful. Ruined by an indelicate notary, he was unable to obtain justice; perhaps it was this misfortune that threw him into the revolutionary party. The author of seditious pamphlets, he was prosecuted at the end of 1789 for grain grabbing and the crime of lèse-nation. Locked up at the Châtelet, Rutlidge was described as a cavalry captain, although he seems never to have belonged to the army.

Released the following year, he gave socialist speeches at the Cordeliers. Rutlidge was a member of the Paris subsistence administration[343] in some capacity. Prosecuted again for causing high grain prices, he was arrested at the same time as Proly and Desfieux. He is thought to have died in prison in 1796[344]. A very long list of his works was published by A. Franklin in his "Vie de Paris sous Louis XVI".

Two wealthy Englishmen staying at the Hôtel Vauban, rue Richelieu, under the names of Milord d'Arck and Chevalier d'Arck, gave sumptuous and mysterious dinners attended by Robespierre, Pétion, Buzot, Prieur, Antoine, Rewbell and Brissot.

One of Pitt's agents, Stanley, was a member of the Mucius Scœvola section[345]. M. A. Mathiez assumes that the same person, under the name of Staley, acted as an intermediary between Perrégaux and the Foreign Office[346].

Faeding, the British government's agent in Calais, is a close

---

[343] *Actes de la Commune de Paris*, t. III.

[344] *The private life of yesteryear* (Franklin).

[345] P. Caron: *Paris during the Terror*.

[346] *Annales révolutionnaires*, August 1916.

friend of Euloge Schneider.

The Irish bootmaker Kavanagh was found at the head of the arms raiders on 13 July 1789; he took part in all the riots and massacres of September. "A coward in the face of peril, he murdered when he could do so without danger"[347].

Mackintosh, a doctor and lawyer, having written an apology for the Revolution, received the title of French citizen from the Legislative Assembly. After reporting his support for the Revolution, he continued to conspire; in 1803, he was prosecuted for inciting the First Consul to murder.

Denis de Vitré, the son of a Canadian man and an English woman, ran a factory belonging to Philippe Égalité. A member of the revolutionary clubs of Paris, Rouen and Montargis, he was denounced to the Jacobins on 16 December 1793 as an agent of Pitt.

Ch. Macdonald is executed as a British spy.

VV.-B. James, a professor of English, was one of the victors of the Bastille; he was appointed secretary of the Jacobin Club. At one time Louis XVI's keeper at the Temple, he seized the king's armchair to prevent him from reading comfortably.

Among the victors of the Bastille were Th. Blackwell, a close friend of Danton, and W. Playfair, author of a plan to manufacture counterfeit money orders to ruin the credit of the Republic.

Hoffmann, Volfmann and Cook appear to be one and the same individual in the list of Dutchmen pensioned by England.

---

[347] Algiers: *Englishmen in the French revolution*, p. 200.

Our Foreign Office was in frequent correspondence with Archibald Mitchell, who was strongly suspected of being one of Pitt's spies.

Lord G. Gordon wrote articles in favour of Cagliostro after the necklace affair, in which he insulted Marie-Antoinette. He was prosecuted and sentenced to five years' imprisonment for insulting the English magistrates. This misadventure prevented him from collaborating with his fellow citizens in Paris in 1789. Gordon left Protestantism to embrace the Jewish religion[348]. This case is rare enough to merit mention.

Baron d'Auerweck was denounced as an agent of both England and Austria. A Hungarian officer, he became an engineer in France; he often came to Paris under the name of Scheltheim.

We have not been able to verify his attitude in 1789. Later, however, he worked with Mrs Atkins to break out prisoners from the Temple and showed devotion to the royal family[349].

It is also difficult to appreciate the role of Lady Kerry. Twice widowed, remarried a third time, she gave plays in her Paris salons. On the eve of 20 June, the Princesse de Lamballe, Messrs de Lage and de Ginestous left her house having lost every penny[350].

Richard Ferris was invited by the Executive Council to come to France and extend his stay for an operation useful to the service of the Republic (21 August 1793).

Captain Frazer, Walsh, Kerny and Mahew are denounced by

---

[348] Burke: *Reflections on the French Revolution.*

[349] F. Barrey: *Mrs Atkins and the Temple Prison.*

[350] R. Arnaud: *The Princess of Lamballe.*

the reports of our diplomatic agents as agents of England.

Among those who attended the Jacobin meetings were J. Stanley of Alderley, Wendham, R. Watt, Wilson Huskisson, Pelham, the future Lord Chichester, and others.

Among the revolutionaries' collaborators were G. Lupton, P. Wentworth, S. Deane, Thomas, Muir, Melvile, O'Drusse, Ghym, Samson Pegnet, editor of a patriot newspaper, etc.[351]

Can it seriously be claimed that such a large number of Englishmen gathered in Paris by chance to work for the overthrow of the monarchy? Alongside the adventurers seeking to take advantage of the disorder to pillage and steal were English officers, literati and former civil servants who had nothing to gain personally from a change of regime in France.

Is it not more likely to believe in an organised plan and to conclude with Robespierre: "these foreigners who try to appear more republican than others are in reality nothing more than agents of the powers"[352].

Alongside the English agents worked a large number of French politicians, suspected of being in the pay of England. No doubt it was convenient to get rid of an adversary by denouncing him as an agent of Pitt, and Robespierre abused this method of government; but all too often his accusations appear to be well-founded.

Chabot claimed that Hébert's wife was an agent of Pitt[353]. We read in Louvet's memoirs (page 9) that Chaumette was, along

---

[351] *Archives nationales*, F. 7, 6468. *Foreign Office Archives*, London, v. 587. Conway: *Paine*. Holland Rose: *W. Pitt.*

[352] Sitting of the Convention, 9 October 1789.

[353] *Annales révolutionnaires*, January 1914.

with Marat, one of the main foreign agents.

When Soulavie was in charge of affairs in Geneva, he collected a certain amount of information on the agents of England, which can be summarised as follows: "Marat took his instructions in London... Clavière was employed to destroy the monarchy by paying the Faubourg Saint-Antoine on 20 June and the Marseillais and others on 10 August... The Troubles in Lyon were paid for by England... Santerre was the distributor of Pitt's gratuities."

According to the secretary of the Committee of General Safety[354], Santerre was responsible for distributing the sums donated by Pitt. English letters announcing the arrival of several million were found at his home.

Dubois Crancé is an accomplice of Dufourny[355]. Lucile Desmoulins is said to have received money from the English government. While Hébert denounced Camille Desmoulins as having sold to Pitt, the Hebertists were condemned on precisely the same grounds. Almost all the revolutionaries hurled the same accusation at each other and one is led to think of the proverb: "There is no smoke without fire".

Other people, who were not bribed by England, were influenced by it, perhaps unconsciously. What mysterious negotiation required Pétion to travel to London with Sillery in order to confer with Pitt[356]? Condorcet and Fox, Brissot and Sheridan were in regular correspondence. Brissot, in love with Madame Macaulay (Catherine Sanbridge), translates her works

---

[354] *Mémoires de Sénar*, p. 10. This accusation is confirmed by Soulavie's diplomatic correspondence.

[355] Buchez and Roux: *Histoire parlementaire*, t. XXXIII, p. 169.

[356] Buchez et Roux, t. XXVI, p. 271.

in which she praises our Revolution.

Lanthenas' speeches were inspired by Pigott and David Williams[357]. Bancal frequents Quakers and Englishmen who collaborate in our Revolution[358]. Roland, Bancal and Lanthenas were so close to Pigott that they planned to settle with him on a vast estate confiscated from the clergy[359].

Roland, Jean-Bon-Saint-André and Barère are members of the Society for Constitutional Information[360].

Mourgues, Minister of the Interior after Roland's departure, wrote in 1792: "My father was brought up in England; I finished my education there. I took my brothers and sister to the area around Bath, where their education is supervised by the part of my family that took refuge in this country when the Edict of Nantes was revoked"[361].

In Chapter XI, we publish documents that lead us to believe that Danton was guilty. In a report recently published by Albert Mathiez, Danton himself stated: "It is quite apparent and proven that the cabinets in London and Vienna may have contributed to the overthrow of the Brissotins"[362].

---

[357] Correspondence with Mme Roland, p. 699.

[358] Correspondance de Mme Roland, p. 743.

[359] Correspondance de Mme Roland, p. 679.

[360] Holland Rose: *W. Pitt*.

[361] *Foreign Office Archives*, London, v. 583.

[362] *Annales révolutionnaires*, April 1916.

CHAPTER X

WHERE THE MONEY COMES FROM

"To deny the influence of foreigners on the French Revolution would be to deny the very evidence", writes M. Hamel[363]. We could say with just as much certainty: to deny the financial sacrifices made by foreigners in favour of the revolutionaries would be to deny the very evidence.

In speaking of *spontaneous* anarchy, Taine seems to be entirely mistaken: most contemporaries of the Revolution mention that the rioters had money in their pockets.

Mirabeau's correspondence reads:

"The death of Foullon cost a hundred thousand livres; that of the baker François a few thousand livres". Bailly shares his opinion.

Danton said to Lavaux at[364]: Hurl with us, *you'll make a lot of money* and then you'll be free to choose your party[365].

---

[363] *Histoire de Robespierre,* vol. III, p. 88.

[364] Sybel: *Histoire de l'Europe,* t. I, p. 96.

[365] The same sentence is recounted in other terms by Chateaubriand, *Mémoires d'outre-tombe.*

During the days of October 1789, Théroigne de Méricour distributed money to soldiers and the populace.

Charles Lameth wrote to Godad on 3 July 1790: "Work with the same zeal; money is not what stops me". A little further on, he added: "We pay the regulars in the galleries (of the National Assembly); we make ourselves applauded by a hundred soldiers whom we decorate with the name of people"[366].

According to Moore, the audience in the galleries, carefully recruited and disciplined, received from four sous to three livres per session. Leaders received between ten and fifty pounds[367].

This is why the most violent speakers were showered with applause, and the moderates greeted with boos. Fearful or indecisive MPs allowed themselves to be swept along by public opinion, unaware that it was rigged.

We don't know," says M. de Bonald, "how much violence, intrigue and money it cost to incite the people to unrest"[368].

A report by Sergeant Marceau to the National Assembly admitted that the Champ de Mars riot "was organised by factious foreigners, paid to sow disorder"[369].

In 1789, the rioters were lured to Paris "by an almost invisible hand that paid for disorder and paid handsomely"[370]. At the time of the October riots, seven million were said to have been sent

---

[366] *Bibliothèque nationale*, L. b. 39, 9040.

[367] Moore: *Views of the French Revolution*, t. I, p. 426.

[368] De Bonald: *Considerations on the French Revolution*, p. 22.

[369] R. ARNAUD: *Fréron's son* (Procès-verbaux de l'Assemblée nationale).

[370] G. Bord: *The storming of the Bastille.*

from abroad.

The distribution of money to the rioters was confirmed by Marmontel, Bezenval, Montjoie, the Marquis de Vergennes and a host of contemporaries. There is disagreement only on the rate of wages, estimated by Lafayette at twelve francs a day, while others speak of six francs. Prices undoubtedly varied from day to day, so the disagreement is only apparent. Mettra, a secret agent of our Ministry of Foreign Affairs, wrote: "It is obvious that the surface of France is covered with secret agitators. When I had my passport stamped on leaving Paris, I saw a man pull out of his pocket two five-pound assignats held together.

People seemed astonished by the wealth of this ragged wretch. This," he replied, "is what was distributed yesterday to the victors of the Bastille"[371].

This testimony was confirmed by foreign diplomats: for example, the Bailli de Virieu, Parma's minister in Paris, wrote on 3 May 1789[372]: "We arrested men in disguise who had their pockets full of gold". The wounded rioters all had between twelve and thirty-six francs on them. One of them moaned: "How can we be treated like this for twelve miserable francs!

Baron de Staël Holstein recounts how a member of parliament made an effort to bring moderation to a group of exalted demonstrators, when a man came up to him and said, showing him twelve francs in his hand: "What you say is true, but your reasons are not worth these[373].

The following year, Staël Holstein reported the arrest in Paris of a Berlin bookseller accused of distributing money to stir up

---

[371] *Foreign Affairs Archives,* Berlin, supplement, no. 9.

[372] Grouchy and Guillois: *The French Revolution as told by a foreigner.*

[373] Diplomatic correspondence of Baron de Staël Holstein.

the people.

Chabroud's report to the National Assembly on the October days speaks of a faction "assured of the delivery of fifteen million per month. The enemies of France were suspected... Forty-five thousand pounds were distributed to the regiment of Flanders; fifty glaziers were enrolled at one louis".

As for the September massacreurs, their salary was one louis per day, payable to the Committee of Four Nations. Documents proving this exist in the papers of Count Garnier[374].

Several historians have claimed that one of the causes of the Revolution was the famine of 1789. But what was the language of the revolutionaries who accused the king of not coming to the aid of his subjects' misery? Of all the ways of stirring up the people," says Alexandre Lameth, "there is none more powerful than presenting them with the image of famine. With two hundred thousand louis, one could in Paris, by making extraordinary purchases, produce alarms whose consequences would be incalculable"[375].

This phrase can be compared to the instructions given to an English agent in 1793: "Maintain high prices and let the traders corner all the essential items"[376].

"Where did Fabre d'Églantine, who was poor before 2 September, get the 12,000 livres in annuities that he confessed to possessing? Where did he get the money to support his hotel, his sail, his people and his daughters? And Lacroix, who has not replied to Guadet's indictment, relating to the negotiation of

---

[374] Mortimer Ternaux: *Histoire de la Terreur*, t. III, p. 275, 521 ff - According to Dr Lebon, some of the massacres were paid twenty-four pounds a day.

[375] G. Bord: *The revolutionary conspiracy of 1789*.

[376] *Archives nationales*, A. D' 108.

millions that the Court had charged him with starting with Pétion? And Panis, and so many others whose sudden fortune dates from September!"[377].

Where did the money come from for Héron who, without any fortune in 1789, was the victim in 1793 of a theft of eight hundred thousand francs worth of securities? Nevertheless, he remained comfortable enough to offer Sénar an annuity of six thousand francs and three thousand six hundred francs in cash, on condition that he rid him of his wife by putting her on a list of suspects.

How did Fournier the American come to own Château de Basancourt in Seine-et-Oise?

According to Mallet du Pan, Hébert left a fortune of more than two million.

Duprat's debts, amounting to sixty thousand francs, were suddenly paid in 1793. In exchange, he was supposed to foment an Anglo-Prussian counter-revolution[378].

Fabre d'Églantine admitted to Marat twelve thousand livres in annuities acquired in one year[379]. Chaumette, an accomplice of Cloots, sent his father large sums attributed to the generosity of Pitt[380]. Barbaroux accused many others; he could have been told that he himself was unable to name the relative who had just bequeathed him eighty thousand francs.

Gonchon, the orator of the Faubourg Saint-Antoine, found

---

[377] Portrait of the Dantonists, by Brissot *(Annales révolutionnaires,* June 1911).

[378] Buchez and Roux: *Histoire parlementaire*, t. XXVI, p. 300.

[379] *Archives nationales*, A. F" 45, register 355.

[380] Buchez and Roux: *Histoire parlementaire*, t. XXXII.

himself in prison with the Countess de Bohm, and admitted that he was paid thirty to forty thousand livres for each riot[381].

According to Sybel, the money needed to maintain the rioting gangs was provided "by speculators such as the Frey brothers, and by the Duc d'Orléans". But the Freys were too practical people to distribute their own money. They could only have been intermediaries acting either on behalf of Freemasonry or on behalf of foreigners.

In 1789, according to some authors, the international Masonic fund had around ten million, and according to others, twenty million. These figures are probably very exaggerated, but the resources of the sect were certainly considerable. Its Grand Master, the Duc d'Orléans, had a magnificent fortune, but the opinion of his contemporaries was that the large sums paid by him accounted for only a very small part of the expenses of the conspiracy.

A revolution in France played into the hands of all governments. We have described Prussia's policy and its plans for expansion in Germany.

The Franco-Austrian agreement worried the House of Savoy. As for Russia, it was preparing, like Prussia, to partition Poland, and the French monarchy was opposed to this. Catherine II, better informed than Louis XVI, was made aware of the plans of Freemasonry and hastened to proscribe it in her states; on the contrary, the preparation of the Revolution in France could not displease her and she once admitted the following: "I am breaking my head to push the courts of Vienna and Berlin to meddle in the affairs of France in order to have a free hand".

---

[381] La Comtesse de Bohm: *Prisons in 1798.* G. Bord: *La conspiration révolutionnaire de 1789*, p. 117.

But the age-old enemy of the French monarchy was England. No other power had so much interest in encouraging riots and civil war in France. Our old rivalry with England had been exasperated by the American War, and the British government was looking for an opportunity to take revenge.

Pitt, who had just come to power, had been brought up by his father to hate France[382]. Auckland admitted that "Great Britain's wish is to reduce France to political nothingness". Chatham believed that his country would "never achieve supremacy of the seas and of commerce so long as the Bourbon dynasty exists". Moreover, Lord Mansfield had dared to declare in Parliament that "money spent in fomenting insurrection in France would be money well spent"[383].

England could pour gold into France without putting too great a strain on its budget, whereas a war entailed risks and could be ruinous. On the other hand, if British finances were in a better situation than ours, the French navy was superior to the An glaise navy.

So, to sum up, the troubles were bribed by an invisible syndicate; England had a great interest in destroying the French monarchy. Is it not worth recalling the old axiom of Roman law: *"Is fecit cui prodest."*

It was, moreover, common knowledge that all the upheavals were fomented and paid for by the British government; in the courts, in the salons, in the clubs, Pitt was accused of being the author of the troubles. Foreign diplomats agreed with our agents on this point. So why did historians deny it? No doubt to save the reputation of the great men of the Revolution. What would become of these heroes if Lafayette's sentence were true:

---

[382] VIDALIN: *William Pitt.*

[383] Sorel: *L'Europe et la Révolution Française*, vol. III, p. 462.

"English money was used to buy Danton, Pétion, Barère, Tallien, Merlin de Douai, Robespierre, Sieyès, etc."[384].

But in such cases proof is very difficult to establish: politicians who sell themselves rarely sign a receipt. A very curious letter, seized from an English agent, contained the following words: "Mylord (Pitt had just been mentioned) wishes you not to think of sending or keeping any account. He even wants all the minutes destroyed, as if they were found they could be dangerous for all our friends in France"[385]. This letter, addressed to the chairman of the English committee in Lille and Saint-Omer, twice recommended that money should not be spared.

According to Granier de Cassagnac[386], a certain number of receipts existed; they were burnt by Savary on the orders of Napoleon Ier. But it seems that these were mainly sums paid by the Duc d'Orléans. In the absence of receipts, correspondence incriminating the guilty parties should have been found. However, it should be noted that every arrest report from 1792 to 1794 mentions the sealing of the accused's papers. There is often mention of numerous letters in English. However, the national archives have not preserved these letters; on the other hand, the accounts of laundresses and tailors have been scrupulously kept. No doubt Savary or others had to clean up their act.

Danton, formally accused by Lafayette, had very warm supporters who defended his honesty. Unfortunately, there is a terrible abundance of evidence against him; Garat, Brissot, Mirabeau, Rœderer, Bertrand de Molleville, Robespierre, Mme Roland, Levasseur, Louis Blanc, Thiers, Mignet, etc., all affirm his venality. Thus M. L. Madelin, in a recent volume, comes to

---

[384] *Mémoires de Lafayette*, t. IV, p. 138. Mathiez : *The days of 5 and 6 October.*

[385] *Archives nationales*, A. D' 108.

[386] Granier de Cassagnac: *Causes of the French Revolution*, p. 146 ff.

this conclusion: "Danton received money from the court and perhaps *from a few* others"[387].

Wouldn't these others be the English? This was rumoured in 1793. M. de la Luzerne, ambassador in London, wrote to M. de Montmorin on November 26, 1790: "There are two Englishmen in Paris, one named Danton, the other Paré, whom some people suspect of being the most particular agents of the English government. Opposite Danton's name, in the margin of the letter, are the words: "Président du d¹ des Cordeliers". But this note is in pencil and in a different handwriting from that of the ambassador[388].

Nevertheless, in the opinion of M. Albert Mathiez[389], it is indeed the famous tribune we are talking about: Paré was, he says, Danton's principal clerk. If the latter was in possession of the letter that we quote on page 231, it is because he was one of England's agents. If M. de la Luzerne believes Danton to be English, it is because his half-brother lived in London and corresponded with him in English. Both, in fact, spoke this language admirably.

As for Robespierre, we have not found any serious documents confirming Lafayette's accusation. But a letter from Charles Lameth clearly establishes that Robespierre was not as independent as his apologists maintained, and seemed to obey the instructions of the occult power: "My friend Robespierre invectives, slanders, that is the way to get nowhere. When can I be rid of this fool? He has just the right amount of common sense to follow the instructions he is given, and with that he always wants to do his bit. It's very sad when fortune forces you to employ people like that. His letter having been interrupted

---

[387] L. Madelin: *La dernière année de Danton* (1914).

[388] *Foreign Office archives*, London, v. 571.

[389] Danton and English gold. *Annales révolutionnaires* of April 1916.

precisely by a visit from Robespierre, Lameth continued in these terms: "The people do not know us, it is even in our dearest interest that they never know us, otherwise the lantern will be out... Work with the same zeal. You know that money is not what stops me, and besides, what reward is promised to you"[390].

The money so generously distributed by Lameth could have come from two sources, England and the Duke of Orleans.

Memoirs of the time are almost unanimous in attributing the first troubles of 1789 to Philippe Égalité [391]. The only controversial point is this: Was he only distributing his own money, or was he also distributing England's money? According to the memoirs of Madame Campan, the ambition of the Duke of Orléans and English gold were the two causes of the Revolution.

Vaudreuil wrote to the Comte d'Artois in 1790: "Soon the royal family will be in the power of a rebel prince supported by the money and forces of England"[392].

"The sums being poured into the people cannot be explained by the very fortune of the Duke of Orléans"[393], said M. de Staël Holstein. It was not enough to pay for the first riots; the leaders of the movement had to be paid from 1789 until 1794.

Rivarol reported the rumour that "the gold distributed by the Duke of Orléans went to the English... We must wait for Mr Pitt to explain the twenty-four million in secret expenditure that he

---

[390] *Letter to Godad,* 3 July 1790, Bibl. nationale, Lb 39, 9040.

[391] The recently published correspondence of Mme de Lostanges once again confirms this evidence. (Letter dated 3 July 1789).

[392] Correspondence from Vaudreuil, 17 June 1790.

[393] Diplomatic correspondence of Baron de Staël Holstein, p. 142.

spoke of in the lower house"[394].

In the unpublished memoirs of the Conventionalist J.-P. Picqué, we read: "Pitt based his project and almost the entire revolutionary system on the Duc d'Orléans"[395].

The opinion of A. Geffroy[396] is that "the faction of the Duc d'Orléans was bribed by England".

On 29 August 1789, the Baron of Staël-Holstein wrote to his government: "England is very likely to be suspected of fomenting and maintaining the troubles. He added on 22 October: "The first party, which must be called a conspiracy rather than a party, has the Duke of Orléans as its leader and England as its driving force"[397].

According to M. Dard, "England, to all appearances, hid its actions behind the Orleanist party"[398].

It seems possible that the Duc d'Orléans ignored the subsidies provided by England to his supporters. Mrs Elliot (Grace Dalrymple), who was of the last good with Philippe Égalité, relates that "the Orleans faction did not even consult him on their operations and used his name to commit horrors"[399]. This opinion explains Camille Desmoulins' joking hypothesis: "Philippe Égalité was perhaps not part of the Orléans faction".

In fact, it was not the Prince who was the head of

---

[394] Rivarol's memoirs.

[395] See *Revue historique de la Révolution Française,* December 1915, p. 271.

[396] *Gustave III* et *la Cour de France,* vol. II, p. 95.

[397] Diplomatic correspondence of Baron de Staël Holstein, p. 142.

[398] DARD: *Choderlos de Laclos,* p. 226.

[399] Memoirs of Mrs Dalrymple-Elliot, p. 37.

Freemasonry, of which he was the Grand Master: he could already have made the admission of an operetta general: "I have to follow them because I am their leader".

No doubt Bezenval (like many others) was right when he spoke in his memoirs of brigands "bribed by the Duke of Orleans and by England". But it would be foolhardy to assert that the Prince had received money from England. It is true that Jefferson expressed the opinion that "the Duke of Orleans is being used as an instrument... the Prince is in league with the court in London. He had no doubt that the ministry would provide him with considerable sums to fuel the civil war"[400].

Jefferson gives no proof of his assertion; Mrs Elliot was more aware than he of the Duke of Orléans' doings, and the 'Orléans faction' could have been paid by the London cabinet without the Prince's knowledge. M. Madelin has announced a biography of Philippe Égalité by M. Britsch; let us hope that it will clarify this point of history when it appears.

However, in the absence of money, the London cabinet lavished promises on the Duke of Orléans, as shown by this sentence in a letter from the Prince: on learning of the illness of the King of England, he wrote: "If George falls completely, you know what Fox and Grenville have promised me; all would be well then"[401].

King Georges had neither sympathy nor esteem for Philippe Égalité, but his ministers lulled the Prince with the hope of a change of dynasty.

In the unpublished memoirs of I.-P. Picqué, deputy for the

---

[400] Jefferson: *Complete Works,* vol. III.

[401] Letter to. Choderlos de Laclos, 10 March 1790. See DESCHAMPS: *Les Sociétés secrètes,* t. II, p. 149.

Hautes-Pyrénées at the Convention, we read: "Pitt was truly the invisible or visible leader of a party directing movements and change opposed to the government...

"England had its confidants and bankers in Basle and Paris, well-styled and widespread agents with the insurrection tariff...".[402]

In his report on the Committee of Public Safety, Cambon wrote: "Since I see Pitt touching five million sterling for secret expenditure, I am not astonished any more that one sows with this money troubles in all the extent of the Republic".

In 1793, Barère denounced the arrival of English spies and agitators in all our departments. Dubois-Crancé reported that William Pitt had sent four million to the Lyon insurgents[403].

We read in Barras' supporting memorandum[404]: "Petitval had bought from Monciel's wife, for a very considerable sum, 25,000 livres I believe, the list of former members of the Convention and the members of the two Councils who were receiving subsidies from England".

William Pitt's methods continued to be used by English diplomats: in 1830, for example, Lieutenant La Roche, in charge of removing the barricade on the Boulevard de la Madeleine, saw Englishmen distributing money to the rioters[405].

It was not only in France that English gold was making

---

[402] *Revue historique de la Révolution Française,* pages 271 to 275.

[403] A. Mathiez : *La Révolution et les étrangers,* Ch. IX.

[404] *Revue Historique,* May 1918 (Article by Doney Lachambaudie).

[405] *Souvenirs d'un officiel de gendarmerie,* published by the Vicomte de Courson. See the article by Félicien Pascal in *l'Echo de Paris,* 1er August 1914.

politicians act. While Fersen declared, with regard to our troubles: "I believe in the arguments of British gold "[406]. Our diplomats wrote from Berlin: "All the people who have access to the King of Prussia are sold to England... The Countess de Bruhl, wife of the Prince Royal's governor, is English and fanatical in her love for her country and her hatred for France... The court physician, a man of great wit, is English"[407].

Eighteen months later, the Marquis de Moustiers said: "Bischoffswerder is being bribed by England"[408].

Bacher, commissioner for foreign relations in Basel, wrote on 19 Thermidor II[409]:

"The Pillnitz Convention and all subsequent arrangements are due to England's gold.

Finally, our diplomatic agents claimed that Thugut had been sold to the English[410].

British influence can be found everywhere: in secret societies as well as in our national assemblies, in clubs and in the Comité de Salut Public, as well as in the ministries of all countries.

---

[406] Lady Blennerhasset: *Mme de Staël and her time*, p. 26.

[407] *Archives des Affaires étrangères,* Berlin, 1789, Letter from M. d'Esterno.

[408] *Foreign Affairs Archives,* Berlin, 10 February 1791.

[409] *Id. in* Berlin, v. 213.

[410] Confidences of Poteratz. Letter from Wickham to Grenville.

CHAPTER XI

ENGLAND AND THE REVOLUTION

In the absence of material evidence, all of the above gives rise to serious presumptions against England. But it was not only public rumour that accused him of bribing troublemakers; it was not only the correspondence and memoirs of contemporaries, but also diplomatic correspondence.

It will be objected that ambassadors who echo the rumours that are circulating can mislead their governments. But when the same fact is asserted in Vienna, London, Paris, Amsterdam, Basle and Berlin, there is a good chance that it is true. The diplomatic correspondence that we publish in the supporting documents can be summed up in this admission by Lord Grenville to Count Stadion: "In order to create useful diversions, the British government is in the habit of maintaining internal disorder on French territory"[411].

Finally, the following letter, seized and translated by order of the Convention, constitutes material proof: it gives instructions from Pitt to the agent in charge of the English committee in Lille and Saint-Omer. It proves that these committees, established in most of our major cities, had been operating for quite some

---

[411] *Manuscripts of J. B. Fortescue*, t. II. Doumic: *Is Freemasonry Jewish or English?* See also the *Memoirs of Barthélemy*, recently published by M. de Dampierre.

time[412]: an agent whose services deserved to be particularly rewarded was promised a seat in parliament.

... "We must make assignats fall more and more. Maintain the high prices and let the traders corner all the essential items...

"Let Chester go from time to time to Ardes and Dunkirk. Once again, don't spare the money...

"See one hundred and fifty thousand francs in Rouen and as much in Caen. Let Mors... be recalled from Cambrai, let Whitmore go to Boulogne[413].

"Mastre should be in Paris, because as a banker he has the best knowledge of how to support the funds and lower the assignats. Milne's plans were approved by Pitt...

"Let no money be spared. Mylord wishes you not to think of sending or keeping any account...

"... If you think Mitchell is safe enough, employ him to go to Paris and Dunkirk... Tell Ness he can be sure of a burg at the first vacancy, or in the next parliament...[414]

"We have forty thousand guineas[415] for the committees under your leadership.

"Don't let Marston stay with you. It is prudent to have separate lodgings..."

---

[412] The letter is dated 29 June 1793.

[413] The words Cambray and Boulogne are crossed out.

[414] Translator's note: i.e. he will be a Member of Parliament.

[415] Translator's note: Nearly six million at the current exchange rate.

Attached to this letter was a list of emissaries designated by initials with the sums to be distributed in fourteen towns: Paris, Rouen, Lille; Nantes, Dunkirk, Calais, Arras, Saint-Omer, Saint-Malo, Boulogne, Douai, Orléans, Blois, Tours[416].

It is hard not to see this document as material proof of the British government's guilt.

According to Barère, documents lost by an Englishman showed that the British government had sent agitators and incendiaries to all our departments.

In fact, fires broke out in Douai, the port of Lorient, Valenciennes, the cartridge factory in Bayonne, the artillery park in Chemillé, and so on.[417]

The Foreign Office has acknowledged that the Prusso-Swiss banker Perrégaux "distributed large sums in Paris in 1793 to various individuals... for the essential services they rendered us"[418].

Here is an official letter from the Foreign Office to the banker Perrégaux, recently published by the *Annales révolutionnaires*[419]:

"We would like you to continue your efforts and to advance 3,000 livres to Mr C. D., 12,000 to W. T. and 1,000 to de M., for the services they have rendered us by breathing fire and bringing

---

[416] *Archives nationales*, A. D' 108, and *Archives des Affaires étrangères*, London, 587.

[417] A. MATHIEZ: *La Révolution et les étrangers*, p. 138.

[418] Lavisse: *La France contemporaine*, t. II, p. 151.

[419] April 1916, A. Mathiez: *Danton and English gold.*

the Jacobins to the height of their fury...

"Help C. discover the channels through which money can be distributed most successfully..."

In publishing this letter, M. Albert Mathiez concludes: "There is no doubt that England maintained agents at the Jacobin who were responsible for pushing the club into demagogic overbidding". As this document forms part of the papers seized from Danton, Mr Mathiez believes that the famous tribune was one of the agents paid by Perrégaux.

In short, if we accept the existence of the English or Angle-Prussian conspiracy, our Revolution is much easier to explain than if we reject this hypothesis.

Let's take a look at the events since the preparation of the Revolution: everything seems to follow logically and the plan of our adversaries is perfectly combined.

From the end of the reign of Louis XV, Brittany was under the influence of emissaries from England. Some malcontents offered the crown to the Duc d'Orléans, father of Philippe Égalité. An army paid by England was to support the movement. When the Duc d'Orléans refused, the conspirators decided to turn to his son; some of them were probably members of the Breton Club, which later became the Jacobin Club. So the British government's support for the ambitions of the younger branch long predated the troubles. Long before the Revolution, the Comte de Vergenne, studying the English question with Louis XVI, had become convinced that "England was working to destroy France through unrest and discord"[420].

The philosophical movement that so skilfully paved the way

---

[420] Campardon: *Le procès du collier.* Soulavie, v. VI, p. 289.

for the fall of the monarchy was launched from abroad. "From Rousseau came Robespierre", writes M. A. Dides [421]. But Rousseau was unquestionably influenced by England and imitated the works of Jacques Thomson.

The writings of the Englishman Locke "served as a preface to the works of Voltaire and Rousseau"[422]. It contains the theories of the souve raineté of the people, the separation of powers, and all the principles of 1789. M. Doumic has also pointed out that the philosophers drew weapons from England against everything they disliked in France: government, religion, customs and the traditional spirit"[423].

If d'Holbach. Helvétius and Diderot were not asking for a republic, they had discredited and weakened royalty, either by insulting it or by undermining Christianity[424].

Helvétius, born in Paris, was of German-Dutch origin. D'Holbach was from Baden. It was in his hotel that libels and pamphlets against religion and royalty were written[425]. They were distributed free of charge in all the provinces. D'Holbach was the introducer of all distinguished foreigners arriving in Paris. Condorcet was his friend and disciple[426]. Helvétius, condemned by the Sorbonne for his book *De l'esprit,* received a warm welcome in Berlin[427]. It was in Mme Necker's salon that it was decided to erect a statue to Voltaire, whose Prussian

---

[421] A. Dide: *Protestantism and the French Revolution*, p. 11.

[422] J. Fabre: *The Fathers of the Revolution.*

[423] Doumic: *The discovery of England in the 18th^e century.*

[424] Aulard: *Histoire politique de la Révolution Française*, p. 11.

[425] J. de Lannoy: *La Révolution préparée par la Franc-maçonnerie*, Omnia Veritas Ltd, www.omnia-veritas.com.

[426] *Grimm's memoirs.*

[427] A. Keim: *Helvétius.*

sympathies were well known. —

The most spiritual people on earth are at the same time the ones who most willingly succumb to foreign influence. Perhaps this is because of the proverb "No man is a prophet in his own country". The Italians had been fashionable during the Renaissance; in the XVIIIe century, it was the English. Louis XVI tried to react against the Anglomania of the courtiers, which made him impatient. One day, when Lauzun was, as was his wont, praising England, the king abruptly told him: "When you love the English so much, you should go and live with them and serve them"[428].

England patiently bided its time while its agents propagated the new ideas and endeavoured to create a revolutionary state of mind in France. The same was true of Prussia.

Our monarchy was in the hands of a sovereign who was weak and indecisive, unable to take sides, and too good to put up vigorous resistance to riots. As early as 1776, Frederick III compared Louis XVI to a young sheep surrounded by old wolves. He was right, and the support he gave to the philosophers was good Prussian policy.

We have already said that French Freemasonry was influenced by England and Germany. Was there a formal agreement between the two governments in London and Berlin? It is probable, but it is impossible to provide proof. Our diplomats and a number of historians affirm that many Prussian figures contributed to the secret funds of the London cabinet. The King of England was brother-in-law to the Duke of Brunswick, and the Berlin court was under British influence.

It was long believed that the Illuminati were exclusively

---

[428] Marquis de Ségur : *Le couchant de la Monarchie*, t. II, p. 219.

German. A recent work by Gustave Bord reveals their links with the English government: "A coterie of Germans *devoted to England* had as accomplices employees of various governments all over the world"[429].

At the end of the reign of Louis XVI, a large number of Englishmen and Germans began to frequent French Masonic lodges, including Lord Stanhope, one of the leaders of English Masonry. In short, the Anglo-Prussian coalition had the formidable force of secret societies and their leaders at its disposal. The British cabinet's ally was the Grand Master of French Freemasonry, the Duc d'Orléans. The royal palace was teeming with spies, and Philippe Égalité could do nothing without the English government being informed.

Ducher, a diplomatic agent, stated in 1793: "For ten years the British Ministry has held the sect of economists at its pledge in France"[430].

At the same time, it was necessary to be able to rely on public opinion; this task was entrusted to the clubs and newspapers. The need for reform was undoubtedly urgent; there were abuses to be eliminated and the philosophers had already been creating a revolutionary mindset for some time. But the action of England accentuated this state of mind throughout France. The constitutionalists, with excellent intentions, found themselves playing into the hands of the international syndicate by unknowingly preparing the overthrow of the monarchy.

We have explained that the Gènevois group, so prominent during the Revolution, was pensioned off by the London cabinet. French Protestants were also under English influence.

---

[429] G. Bord: *Les Illuminés de Bavière* (Revue des Société secrètes).

[430] *Foreign Office Archives,* London; 587.

The movement for freedom of the press was launched by David Williams; the Declaration of the Rights of Man was the work of Thomas Paine; the inventor of the red bonnet was Robert Pigott. The clubs imported to France from England worked on public opinion alongside the secret societies. After the political club, founded in 1782, the American club was created in 1785 by the Duc d'Orléans. Several other circles also began to discuss political issues. They worried the government and were all closed down in 1787. The law of 14 December 1789 gave them the right to reopen, but they had not waited for permission, since as early as June, and perhaps earlier, the famous Breton club was meeting in Versailles[431]. We know that it later became the Jacobin Club when it moved to the convent in the rue Saint-Honoré[432]. Did the police ignore the meetings of the Breton Club? It is likely that they turned a blind eye.

After the Club Breton, a fairly large number of clubs opened where gambling was replaced by politics, such as the Foreigners' Club, in the rue de Chartres; the Colonists' Club, founded by the Americans; the Lazowski Society, created later by the Americans, and so on.

The English element dominated the *Friends of Blacks* club, which played a fairly important role.

"As early as December 1790, the Jacobins club included notorious foreigners among its members, many of whom were not even domiciled"[433]. At the Cordeliers, a large number of Swiss fraternised with Marat, including Virchaux, Niquille,

---

[431] He was already corresponding with all the regiments to encourage them to desert. See Aulard: *La Société des Jacobins*, t. I. Introduction, p. 20 ff.

[432] The entrance door still exists, on rue Saint-Hyacinthe, 4, behind the Marché Saint-Honoré.

[433] Mathiez: *The Revolution and Foreigners*, p. 42.

Roullier, d'Arbelay and Chaney[434].

The Constitutional Society went unnoticed. Burke, in his reflections on the French Revolution, was astonished that the recognition of our compatriots went only to the "Revolution society" and not at all to the Constitutional society "which has been working for seven or eight years in the same direction" (1er novembre 1790).

This English association, which has been ignored by historians, had been preparing for the Revolution since 1783.

The Friends of the People Society was entirely English, like its predecessor[435]. Lord Grey was one of its leading members.

The cercle Social, on the other hand, where Abbé Fauchet and Nicola Bonneville shone, seemed French. But Anacharsis Cloots and Thomas Paine were editors of its newspaper, the *Iron Mouth*. *The* aim of the cercle Social was to centralise Freemasons, eliminating all reactionary elements. The cercle Social admitted women; Mme d'Aelders, an agent of the Prussian government, was a member, along with a number of elegant women who frightened the austere Jacobins[436]. Bonneville's proposal was therefore rejected when he wanted to merge the cercle Social with the Jacobin club[437]. Les Amis de la vérité was an offshoot of the cercle Social; Mme d'Aelders tried to found the patriotic society of Les *Amies* de la vérité at the same time.

The Nomophiles club, on rue Saint-Antoine, also had

---

[434] See the list of foreigners belonging to the Jacobin Club below.

[435] Peyrat: *The French Revolution*, p. 146.

[436] It was inaugurated in the Palais-Royal circus.

[437] A. Jouet: *Clubs.*

members of both sexes; Théroigne de Méricour shone brightly[438].

Many foreigners were regulars at the Cordeliers club, the most violent of all: Rutledge, Dufourny, Desfieux, Dubuisson, Proly, etc.

The English revolutionary club, presided over by Stone, played a most active role in the French Revolution. A list of its members cannot be found, but here are the names of the Englishmen who dined there on 18 November 1792: Thomas Paine, the banker R. Smith, Rayment, Frost, Sayer, Joyce, H. Redhead, Yorke and R. Merry, husband of the actress Miss Brunton.

The English revolutionary club had been created by the Revolution Society, whose headquarters were in London. The main leaders of the Revolution Society were Lord Stanhope, who is to be found everywhere, and Dr Price. The latter, after the October days, thanked God for having made him alive enough to see these events. Burke tells us that what excited the enthusiasm of the Revolutionary Society was the cry: "Bishops to the lantern".

The correspondence of the Revolution Society with the French clubs forms a rather rare volume bearing the words: "Strictly prohibited in England". It contains letters from a large number of Jacobin societies, thanking them for the advice they had received; indeed, the English Revolutionary Society was a constant source of inspiration for our assemblies; it was in correspondence not only with Paris, but with all our major cities, which sent patriots to London to meet Lord Stanhope. As early as 1788, the Revolution Society had proclaimed the immortal principles that our revolutionaries claim to have invented: freedom of conscience, freedom of the press, sovereignty of the

---

[438] Isambert: *Life in Paris*, 1791–1792.

people, the right to insurrection, etc. The Revolution Society was also a source of inspiration for our assemblies.

According to the Duchesse de Brissac [439], the Landre *Correspondence Society* consisted of six thousand people headed by a secret committee of six unnamed members.

Some political salons collaborated with the clubs: that of Mm de Condorcet, frequented by the English and by Cloots, those of Mme François Robert, of the banker Kornmann, and so on.[440]

As soon as the Revolution began, the international conspiracy set out to monopolise the press, whose power was beginning to make itself known. The Englishman Rutledge published the *Fortnight.* The *Courrier de l'Europe* belonged to his compatriot Swinton. The Society of Black Friends, bribed by England, published *the Observateur.* Thomas Paine inspired Brissot's articles and wrote La *Bouche de fer* with Anacharsis Cloots. *L'Union,* inspired by Robespierre, appeared in both English and French. Oswald was one of the founders of the *Chronique du mois.* At the same time, Von der Goltz's diplomatic correspondence mentions the *Journal National,* subsidised by him in Paris, being sent to Berlin[441]. The Prussian Cloots inspired the articles by Camille Desmoulins; the Austrian Proly contributed to the *Cosmopolite.* The Milanese Gorani wrote for the *Moniteur.* The Prussian Z. Hourwitz contributed to several newspapers. The Italians Pio and Ceruti were editors of the *Feuille Villageoise* and the *Journal de la Montagne.* Prince Ch. de Hesse edited the *Journal des hommes libres.* Dumont from Genoa contributed to Le *Républicain.* His fellow citizen Clavière published the *Chronique du mois* and wrote for the *Courrier de*

---

[439] Duchesse de Brissac: *Pages sombres,* p. 179.

[440] Under the Directoire, the Cercle Constitutionnel, chaired by Benjamin Constant, was founded to combat the royalist Cercle de Clichy.

[441] *Foreign Affairs Archives,* Berlin, v. 212.

Provence. The Belgian F. Robert was editor of the *Mercure* and the *Révolutions de Paris.* We should also mention La Harpe, D^r Kœrner, Cotta (from Stuttgart), Dorsch (from Mainz), the Savoyard Dessaix, etc. The newspaper Le *Creuset* was edited by Rutledge; Dessonaz from Genoa edited the *Correspondance des Nations* with Grenus; Euloge Schneider edited *the Argus* in German. Revolutionary English newspapers appeared in Paris, including the *Magazine of Paris and* the *Paris Mercury.* The Club Helvétique published the *Correspondance générale Helvétique.* Rebmann published *Die Schilwache and* Die Geissel in Paris; he collaborated with the Prince of Hesse on the *Journal des Campagnes* and the *Ami des lois.*

In parallel with the Prussian intrigues, British agents had long been working to discredit Marie-Antoinette in order to dissolve the Franco-Austrian entente.

Ambassador Dorset, who had the Queen's confidence, was himself stirring up discord at the Court of Versailles. After the affair with the necklace, Cagliostro was well received in London, where he had not left a good reputation. When he was later imprisoned for debts, an Englishman got him out again.

"At the signal of the convocation of the Estates General, provoked surreptitiously by the accomplices and emissaries of her minister, England unfolded upon us the infernal plot that she had woven in the shadows and in silence"[442]. A swarm of English agents had gradually settled in France to direct the prepared movement. We have quoted the letter establishing the existence of committees in fourteen towns. But, of course, it was mainly in Paris that they were active. Barère wrote in one of his reports: "The English have from Dunkirk to Bayonne and from Bergues to Strasbourg secret corrupters and intelligences in the

---

[442] *Archives des Affaires étrangères,* England, supplement, v. 15. Durban's report to the Directoire.

garrisons".

A few days after the storming of the Bastille, Dorset was in a singular hurry to inform M. de Montmorin of a so-called plot by aristocrats to surrender Brest to the English. He could not name the perpetrators for one very good reason: the plot did not exist. But he seemed, or appeared, to be more sincere when he denied any responsibility for our first troubles. Moreover, wasn't the way in which the British government exonerated itself likely to arouse our suspicions rather than dispel them: The king of England protests that he has nothing to do with the disorders in Paris; Grenville repeats this insistently[443]. Ambassador Dorset, not content with asserting this to Louis XVI, wrote two letters to the President of the National Assembly to exonerate himself. It must be said that appearances were against him. But this time, the London cabinet understood that Dorset was exaggerating, and blamed him for having written to the President of the Assembly.

The English historian Holland Rose has discovered a proof of the sincerity of his Government: it is that not one of King George's letters to his ministers or ambassadors even alludes to the French Revolution. He who wishes to prove too much proves nothing: who is to believe that an event of this importance went unnoticed in London? On the contrary, our diplomatic agents state that the King of England "never stops talking about the Revolution". Can we assume that he does not talk about it to his ministers and ambassador? However, as British diplomacy has always remained in the hands of career men, its secrets have not been divulged by demagogues and parvenus. One objection can be made to the hypothesis of the Anglo-Prussian plot, and that is that proof of it should be found in the London archives. A sentence from the *Mémorial de Sainte-Hélène*[444] answers this objection: "All the English political agents are in a position to

---

[443] *Foreign Office Archives,* London, v. 578.

[444] V. IV, p. 262.

make two reports on the same subject, one public and false for the ministerial archives, the other confidential and true for the ministers alone".

Pitt once told Lord Stanhope: "Whatever we have to spend, we must spare nothing to start a civil war in France"[445].

We have already quoted Lord Grenville's admission. Lord Mansfield also dared to tell Parliament that the money spent on fomenting insurrection in France would be money well spent[446]. The Duke of Bedford later admitted to the House of Lords[447]: "Our efforts have greatly contributed to the establishment of the regime of Terror in France, and our ministry has had a great share in the misfortunes that have befallen it"[448].

M. de Montmorin wrote with a great deal of good sense at the beginning of the Revolution: "The troubles which are stirring up the kingdom are attracting the attention of all the powers, and most of them see them with a secret joy… Among these powers we must distinguish Great Britain… We know that the desire to weaken France is the first m bile of politics".

Montmorin admitted that he could not find precise proof, because, he said, by 13 August, "the police no longer existed. But what is certain is that the money was spread with the greatest profusion amongst the soldiers and the people"[449].

---

[445] HAMEL: *Histoire de Saint-Just,* p. 422.

[446] Sorel: *L'Europe et la Révolution,* vol. III, p. 462.

[447] 27th January 1795.

[448] It goes without saying that the actions of English ministers one hundred and thirty years ago cannot diminish the debt of gratitude contracted by France in 1914 towards the great nation that came to our aid to repel the invasion of the Barbarians from across the Rhine.

[449] *Foreign Office archives,* London, v. 570.

M. de La Luzerne replied to Montmorin that our first troubles were most likely fomented by Dorset.

The first sparks of our Revolution," said Napoleon I[er], "and all the horrible crimes that followed, were the work of Pitt… Posterity will recognise him… This man, so highly praised in his day, will one day be nothing more than the genius of evil"[450].

The October Days were undoubtedly organised by the English government with the help of the Duc d'Orléans. Diplomatic correspondence bears this out as well as contemporary accounts. After these days, Lafayette had the Duc d'Orléans sent on a mission to England. The idea was perhaps not a very happy one, since the prince appeared to be conspiring with the help of that country; but above all the court wanted to get him away from Paris. Philippe-Égalité was instructed to search London for the authors of the troubles—a task that should not be very difficult for him. —Lafayette told him: "You are more interested in this than anyone else, because no one is as involved as you are"[451]. Lafayette then suggested to the Prince that if he refused to go to London he might well be arrested.

Our ambassador in London, M. de la Luzerne, was asked to keep an eye on the Duc d'Orléans. The English ministers remarked to him that the Prince was "leaving France rather out of necessity than of his own free will".

M. de La Luzerne protested against such an idea with the same assurance as the English minister when they claimed to be strangers to our troubles. In the words of Beaumarchais, "Who is being deceived here?

La Luzerne wrote on 30 November: "I am trying to find out

---

[450] *St Helena Memorial*, v. VII, p. 218.

[451] Louis Blanc, t. III, p. 250.

if, instead of talking to the English ministers about the affairs of the Netherlands, the Duke of Orléans is not conspiring with them to stir up new troubles in France... But the King and Mr Pitt have such a low opinion of the Duke of Orléans, they believe him to be so unsuited to be the leader of a party, that they will not mix their affairs with his. I cannot tell you how much the arrival of this Prince has given the English of all classes a bad opinion of him...

"The Duc d'Orléans never talks to me about his visits to the English ministers, which I know are very frequent"[452].

A few months later the Prince, bored in London, asked to return to Paris, unless he was appointed ambassador instead of La Luzerne. This insinuation met with no success.

For the anniversary of 14 July, the English government foresaw serious disorder, and the Prince of Wales urged the Duke of Orléans to return to Paris to attend[453].

In denouncing the Duc d'Orléans' plans to the Assembly, Ribes, deputy for the Pyrénées-Orientales, claimed that the Prince had concluded the following arrangement: He would abandon our colonies to England in exchange for the support of the British government, which was to push him to the throne[454]. Ribes pointed out the frequent trips made by Talleyrand and Philippe Égalité to London, and the newspaper articles paid for by the Société des Amis des Noirs. But the Duc d'Orléans was defended by Robespierre, Danton, Marat and the Cordeliers[455]. Ill-intentioned people assumed with some probability that the

---

[452] *Foreign Office archives,* London, v. 571 and 572.

[453] *Foreign Affairs Archives*, London 573 and 574.

[454] Pallain: *Talleyrand's Mission to London*, p. 345 and 346.

[455] Bouillé's memoirs. Memoirs by Louvet.

support of these characters was not disinterested.

After the flight from Varennes, Fox declared that the time had come to abolish royalty in France[456]. In September 1791, Mercy Argenteau told our ambassador that England had fomented our first disorders and would continue until total ruin[457]. Worontzof was irritated by the blindness of Russia and Spain "who do not see England's activities in France"[458]. And our ambassador in London wrote: "England no longer has anything to fear from France and can without fear arrogate to herself supremacy in the two Worlds".

The Duke of York's candidacy for the throne began to be discussed timidly in Paris.

The second son of the King of England, the Duke of York had married a princess of Prussia, and this marriage, says M. Aulard, "had made him sympathetic to the patriots"[459]. The secret committee of the Jacobins, on the proposal of Manuel and Thuriot, decided in 1792 to replace Louis XVI with either the Duke of York, the Duke of Brunswick or Philippe Égalité[460]. Carra supported the Duke of York's candidacy at the Jacobin Club[461].

The following year, General Wimpffen, a deputy from Caen, again proposed asking England for a king[462]. A detachment of the Valenciennes garrison spread the word that the Duke of York,

---

[456] E. Champion: *L'esprit de la Révolution Française*, p. 200.

[457] *Foreign Office Archives*, London, 578.

[458] *Id.* v. 579.

[459] AULARD: *Histoire politique de la Révolution. Française*, p. 254.

[460] G. Bord: *Autour du Temple*, t. I, p. 191 and 578.

[461] *Archives nationales*, A. F'', 45, reg. 355.

[462] Aulard: *Histoire politique* de *la Révolution Française*, p. 897.

who alone could make France happy, should be brought to the throne. English money was found in the soldiers' pockets.

Montgaillard claimed to have been entrusted by Robespierre with negotiations with the Duke of York. We read in Garat's memoirs: "The Jacobins, who seem to be leading France, are being led by the Cordeliers; the Cordeliers are preparing to shed streams of blood to bring out a new throne (the Duke of York)".

A letter from Noël, our diplomatic agent in London, calmed the enthusiasm of the English Prince's supporters. Some people," he wrote, "seemed convinced that serious thought was being given to offering the crown to the Duke of Brunswick. I do not know the intentions of the Assembly and the Council. But, if France is not disgusted with kings, I believe it is my duty to tell you what I have learned about the Duke of York, about whom you know that some French papers have spoken in the same vein. Fierce to the point of beating soldiers to death with sticks, bloodthirsty, talentless, witless, drunk every day, the horror and contempt of the English nation, he has never shown any honest or humane inclination, and the poor health of the Prince of Wales makes us glimpse with dread the moment when such a man will be king".[463]

The Duke of York's supporters soon rallied behind the Duke of Brunswick's candidacy, which was defeated by the Orleans faction.

The poor harvest and food shortages were exploited by the leaders of the Revolution to stir up the people. The English government took advantage of the situation to make substantial purchases of wheat and flour in France, thereby aggravating the

---

[463] *Foreign Office Archives,* London, v. 582.

situation[464].

In his speech on 8 Thermidor, Robespierre told the Convention that "famine is the result of England's actions"[465].

Cambon's report to the Salut Public committee also accused foreigners of being responsible for the crisis and attributed the fall in assignats to Pitt's actions[466].

At the time of the days of 20 June and 10 August, when the armed groups were forming, agents from the English Ministry were scattered around to stir them up[467].

It is worth noting that Lord Gower had already announced to London on 4 August that the Tuileries would soon be attacked. Lord Grenville replied: "Express to the King our feelings of friendship and goodwill, but *nothing in writing*". The London cabinet was obviously neutral.

According to M. de Montmorin, almost all those who forced their way into the Tuileries on 20 June were foreigners.

Several Englishmen sent money to the widows of patriots killed on 10 August[468]; others sent money to rioters wounded during the insurrection.

The massacres of September were not, writes Lindet, the

---

[464] On this subject, see the Memoirs of the flag-bearer Orson, published by F. CASTANIÉ.

[465] Robespierre's speeches and reports, p. 420.

[466] MATHIEZ: *La Révolution et les étrangers,* p. 136.

[467] Biré: *Journal d'un bourgeois de Paris.*

[468] *Recueil de Tuetey*, t. IV, 2911 and 2950.

result of a popular movement: "Everything was ordered"[469]. (This is a revolutionary speaking, not a reactionary.) Danton and Camille Desmoulins had announced the massacres before they had begun.

During those dreadful days, two Englishmen in frock coats poured glasses of wine for the assassins, telling them: "Be strong and courageous"[470].

The salary of the massacreur was one louis per day; some received twenty-four francs.

These massacres, being both clumsy and cruel, could only harm the revolutionary cause. If, therefore, the foreign syndicate really was the instigator, the only plausible explanation seems to us to be the following: it wanted to discredit the men who were beginning to become too powerful, and at the same time to make the moderates revolt against the Jacobins.

The King of England was obviously torn between two feelings: he wanted the French monarchy to fall, but he feared the contagion of revolutionary ideas. In any case, he probably did not want Louis XVI to die.

But Pitt was ruthless: during secret negotiations with the Convention, Danton declared himself ready to save the king in return for a million to be distributed skilfully among his colleagues; Théodore Lameth passed the proposal on to Pitt, who refused [471]. The judgement was handed down before the monarchists had time to raise the requested sum elsewhere. It is

---

[469] Madelin: *The French Revolution*, p. 260

[470] Papers of Marquis Garnier. Declaration by citizen Jourdan, former president of the Petits-Augustins district. Memoirs of Montgaillard. Collection of memoirs on the French Revolution.

[471] Lord Acton: *Lectures on the French Revolution.* Holland Rose: *Pitt,* p. 94.

impossible to know whether William Pitt kept the proposal secret or communicated it to his sovereign.

Talon, former criminal lieutenant at the Châtelet, made the following statement to Charles Lameth[472]: "Pitt wants the King of France dead. Nothing that I have been able to express has moved or shaken him. Danton vouches for the salvation of Louis XVI if England is willing to add two million to what the knight Ocariz can dispose of[473] … Pitt wants in France the counterpart of Charles Ier."

Talon repeated this testimony before the consular court: Pitt and the foreign powers refused to make the financial sacrifices demanded by Danton to save the king.

When Talon was distributing the monarchy's secret funds, he took Danton into his service; the famous tribune gave him a passport to emigrate[474].

The Irishman Thomas Whaley, who travelled in France during the Revolution, recounts the following anecdote in his memoirs:

"On 21 January, some of my compatriots entered the café and, with an air of perfect self-satisfaction, showed me their handkerchiefs which they had obtained permission to dip in the King's blood.

The Duc d'Orléans had formally promised Mrs Dalrymple

---

[472] G. Rouanet: *Danton and the death of Louis XVI* (Annales révolutionnaires, January-February 1916).

[473] Minister of Spain.

[474] MATHIEZ: *Danton et la mort du Roi* (Annales révolutionnaires, June 1922, p. 235-236).

Elliot not to vote for the death of Louis XVI[475]. It is probable that he was forced to do so by Freemasonry; the shame and remorse he felt about it seem to have been the cause of his resignation as Grand Master. By leaving the sect, Philippe Égalité lost all his influence and was sidelined until he was prosecuted and guillotined.

The Bourbon monarchy had been destroyed; England had won the first part. Burke drew the following conclusion from the events: "The French have overthrown their monarchy, their church, their nobility, their laws, their army, their navy, their trade... They have done our business better than twenty Ramillies"[476].

After the fall of Louis XVI's throne, the English government did not remain inactive. The following document seized by the French police is proof of this:

"The King of France is dead; what does it matter to us? Our only aim is to shrink France, to destroy it, so that it will no longer be a balance in the political equilibrium...

"We must raise different parties, lead them all, organise anarchy, etc..."

But the death of Louis XVI signalled a U-turn in the foreign syndicate's plan. The original aim of the Revolution had been achieved; the fire ignited in Paris now threatened to spread throughout Europe. On learning of Louis XVI's arrest at Varennes, the King of Prussia had already exclaimed: "What a terrible example!"[477] . In England, revolutionary clubs were modelling themselves on ours; it was imprudent to encourage

---

[475] Memoirs of Mrs Dalrymple Elliot, p. 37.

[476] STANHOPE; *William Pitt.*

[477] *Foreign Affairs Archives,* Berlin, v. 212.

new ideas. In addition, the armies of the Convention were proving to be much more formidable than Europe had anticipated; and yet our main generals had been proscribed, Lafayette, Dillon, Dumouriez, Custine, Biron, Montesquieu, Valence, Houchard, Miaczinki, and so on.

From then on, England's policy tended to diminish the strength of the Republican party; consequently, the order was given to favour not the Jacobin plots, but the royalist plots and the insurrections of the Chouans and the Vendéens. Four million euros were sent to Lyon for the same purpose by the London cabinet.

According to Barbaroux, Pitt's plan was to restore the monarchy in the north, leaving the south of France as a republic. He would then help the southern republic to fight the northern monarchy[478].

Among the efforts to be encouraged was obviously the conspiracy of Jean de Batz. The sums spent by this extraordinary character seem too large to have come solely from his personal fortune and, at the time of Louis XVI's death, the royalist coffers were not very well-stocked. As the English bankers Boyd and Kerr were among Jean de Batz's agents, it is safe to assume that they were the intermediaries for the advances made by the British government to fight the Convention. Here, according to the national archives[479], is the list of the main agents of the famous conspirator:

Proli.

Pereira.

Desfieux, wine merchant.

---

[478] *National archives,* A. F" 45.

[479] *Id. at* F. 7, 4774, 67.

Dufourny de Villiers, administrator of poudres et salpêtres.

Gusman.

Guyot Desherbiers, judge at the Civil Court.

Lullier, public prosecutor.

Noël, Commissioner.

Varlet, Fournerot, Chapelle, apaches.

Burlandeux, policeman.

Frei, Jewish banker.

Gauge, stock market broker.

Benoist.

Boyd.

Kerr.

Dulac,

Dossonville,   police officers.

Marino,

Dangerous,

Soulès,

Coldness,

The Vienna cabinet seems to have had exactly the same plan as Jean de Batz. Hefflinger's confidences and the correspondence of Jeanneret, the diplomatic agent, bear this out[480].

Once in power, the leaders of the Revolution seemed surprised by their success and immediately showed great disarray. In the words of Joseph de Maistre, they did not lead events; they were led by them. "There is something passive and

---

[480] See chapter X.

mechanical about the seemingly most active figures of the Revolution. Mediocre men like Robespierre, Collot d'Herbois or Billaut Varennes were the most astonished by their power"[481].

Isn't it always the invisible hand whose action we pointed out?

With the revolutionary government on the road to bankruptcy, the English ministers had factories of counterfeit assignats set up to precipitate financial panic. This fact, reported by our diplomatic agents[482], was denounced by Sheridan in the House of Commons (sitting of 18 March 1793).

Pitt's diplomacy had armed most of the powers of Europe against France while observing an apparent neutrality—that was acting skilfully. —But after the execution of Louis XVI, the British government made our ambassador surrender his passports. The Convention hesitated at first to respond to this insult with a declaration of war. Then, if Maret (the future Duke of Bassano) is to be believed, a number of high-ranking men, having played the game to the downside, made a definitive break with England[483].

At the outbreak of hostilities, the English residing in France were preparing to leave, when the British Ministry invited them to remain on the continent, unless special permission was granted: they were too useful! The Conventionalists were so much in the hand of England that they did not object at first. But there were so many denunciations against the English and the members of the government bribed by them that it became difficult to turn a blind eye: on 19 October 1793, the Convention

---

[481] J. de Maistre: *Considerations on France,* p. 10.

[482] *Foreign Office Archives,* London, supplement, v. 15. Report on the British Cabinet message.

[483] Correspondence of W. A. Miles, p. 86.

voted to arrest all foreigners whose governments were at war with France.

Robespierre nevertheless asked for exceptions to be made on the grounds that "a certain number of them held public office with honour"[484].

This decree made the task of the Anglo-Prussian syndicate much more difficult. But a few good secret agents were able to continue to do favours for French politicians.

Prussia's actions seem to have gone unnoticed in Paris; moreover, Ephraim and Cloots had not been replaced. On the other hand, Barère and Camille Desmoulins repeatedly denounced England: in his report of 6 March 1793, Barère repeated that Pitt had bribed the riots in France; he added that he did not wish to make any further revelations[485]. This was no mystery to anyone. Garnier therefore proposed that the Convention decree that everyone had the right to assassinate Pitt. But the Assembly was content to decree that Pitt was "the enemy of the human race"[486]. The English minister does not seem to have been otherwise moved.

Before the proscription of foreigners, eight or ten Englishmen "collaborated with and led the Jacobins"[487].

Was it a question of voting? So few voters dared to go to the polls that votes were easy to change. The moderates did not take part in the vote; thus, the proportion of abstentions in the election of the General Council of the Paris Commune was 95%. The

---

[484] Hamel: *Histoire de Robespierre*, t. III, p. 189.

[485] See among others: BLIARD: *Les Conventionnels régicides*, p. 143 ff.

[486] Buchez and Roux: *Histoire parlementaire*, tome XXXVIII. *Moniteur* du 9 août 1793.

[487] Papers of Lord Auckland, 4 September 1792.

number of voters in the election of the Mayor of Paris was 71.5%. Under these conditions, votes don't cost much to buy. As for the public in the galleries, representing the opinion of the people, we have given the figures for their salaries.

We have not been able to discover what became of the eight or ten Englishmen mentioned by Lord Auckland after the decree against foreigners. The only one whose name has been admitted is Auguste Rose, reported as one of the "ten overseers of the Convention"[488].

It is likely that Fox was in constant contact with the Jacobins. For example, when Mrs Elliot, a friend of Philippe Égalité, was arrested, the Revolutionary Court accused her of being in correspondence with Fox. She replied, "Isn't Mr Fox a friend of the Supervisory Committee?"[489] .

In the indictment of the Hebertists we read: "The English government and the coalition powers are the leaders of this conspiracy[490].

A report by Barère states that "the English have, from Dunkirk to Bayonne and from Bergues to Strasbourg, secret corrupters and intelligence officers in the garrisons"[491].

Robespierre fought ceaselessly against England, denouncing Pitt's actions and indiscriminately proscribing all citizens suspected of pacting with foreigners. He was becoming too powerful and too troublesome; the Anglo-German coalition tried to overthrow him and encouraged the reactionary movement of 9

---

[488] ALGER: *Englishmen in the French Revolution,* p. 195 ff.

[489] Memoirs of Mr.me Dalrymple Elliot, p. 127. Duchesse de Brissac: *Dark pages.*

[490] Buchez et Roux, t. XXXI, p. 364.

[491] Buchez et Roux, t. XXXIII, p. 118.

Thermidor. It was the Englishman A. Rose was responsible for taking Robespierre prisoner to the Comité de Salut Public.

The hand of the foreigner is still to be found in the disorders known as the White Terror. Undoubtedly, a certain number of royalists wanted to avenge their relatives and friends who had been guillotined, but in many places the rioters were the same revolutionaries who used to massacre royalists in the name of the republic, and who now massacred republicans, claiming to be Thermidorian[492]. They undoubtedly had a motive for acting in this way; is it not natural to suppose that this motive was none other than the usual salary of rioters?

After the victories of the Republican armies, emigration had pinned its hopes on the conspiracies hatched by agents, "most of whom are paid handsomely from English funds"[493].

When, on the death of Louis XVII, the émigrés proclaimed the Count of Provence king (24 June 1795), William Pitt sent him a secret ambassador, Lord Macartney. The support of the British cabinet had, it is said, been offered in 1789 to the Duc d'Orléans in exchange for our colonies; it was offered in 1796 to the Comte de Provence, again in exchange for our colonies, and also on condition of a rectification of the borders in the Netherlands. Louis XVIII was indignant and hastened to publish the declaration of Verona to cut short Pitt's intrigues. His righteousness deprived him of powerful help. As Hyde de Neuville observed, the British government's game consisted in "holding the republic in check, maintaining resistance just enough to prolong it, but not helping it effectively enough to make it victorious"[494].

---

[492] See Buchez and Roux: *Histoire parlementaire,* t. XXXVI, p. 411.

[493] Trudeau Dangin: *Royalists and Republicans.*

[494] Memoirs of Hyde de Neuville, p. 242.

In 1795, the agents of the London cabinet boasted that they were able to dispose of the anarchists, organise "days" and make a profit from them[495]. As they did not always agree with the agents of the Princes, who thwarted them and sometimes denounced them, the English government took revenge on them in Brittany.

In the souvenirs of an émigré (Comte de Coetlogon) recently published by the *Revue hebdomadaire*[496], we read: "I saw clearly that England and the other kings of Europe only wanted to prolong the troubles in France and wait for the favourable moment when its convulsions would have weakened it, in order to be able to dismember it more easily".

Throughout the Revolution, the émigrés were England's dupes. I had no trouble," said Hoche, "convincing Cormatin that the Chouans, the Vendéens and the émigrés had been played by the coalition and in particular by England"[497].

Vaudreuil tried in vain to open the eyes of the Count of Artois: "I see you," he wrote to the Prince, "still fooled by Pitt's assurances, and that distresses me. I cannot believe in the help of the man most interested in our loss and whom I still believe to be the main architect of it"[498].

The deplorable inertia of the Princes while their partisans were being killed in Brittany and the Vendée has been criticised with some justification. But it must be admitted that England was mainly responsible.

---

[495] Sorel: *L'Europe et la Révolution Française,* vol. IV, p. 350.

[496] 12 August 1922, p. 225.

[497] H. WELSCHINGER: *Le Baron de Cormatin,* p. 44.

[498] Correspondence from Vaudreuil, 3 July 1790.

Sometimes the London cabinet was frankly opposed to the landing of the Count of Provence and the Count of Artois on the French coast, sometimes it found pretexts to delay the operation from week to week. From time to time, he considered the life of the pretender too precious to expose in Brittany. Then, after having promised an army, he limited himself to sending false assignats to the Vendée.

Napoleon Ier expressed the following opinion on this subject: "If English policy had allowed a French prince to take control of the Vendée, that would have been the end of the Directoire"[499].

What is more, it is clear from a confession made by Napoleon to General d'Andigné (on 27 December 1799), that in this case he would have restored royalty: "if the Princes had been in the Vendée, I would have worked for them"[500].

My inactivity," wrote the Count of Provence to the Duke of Harcourt, "gives my enemies the opportunity to slander me. It even exposes me to unfavourable judgements from those who have remained loyal to me, judgements that I cannot call rash, since those who make them are not instructed in the truth"[501].

M. Gautherot, in an interesting work on *the Vendée Epic,* gives precise details of the duplicity of the English government towards the French royalists. At certain times, pilots were forbidden, on pain of death, to take emigrants wishing to join the Vendéens to France.

For its part, Austria also endeavoured to thwart Louis XVIII's

---

[499] Mémorial de Sainte-Hélène. Memoirs of Hyde de Neuville, p. 234.

[500] H. WELSCHINGER: *Le Baron de Cormatin,* p. 32.

[501] L. Sciout: *Le Directoire,* t. I, p. 332 et seq. See also the diplomatic correspondence published at the end of this volume (Pièces justificatives, p. 276).

efforts: when the pretender took the lead of the émigrés, the court in Vienna informed him that if he did not leave the army immediately, measures would be taken to force him to do so[502].

Lord Grenville told Earl Stadion:

"We give all the French parties hopes that commit us to nothing, in order to maintain and foment internal unrest."

Under the Directoire, the English agent Wickham centralised correspondence with royalists throughout France in Basel. He helped them in their plots, depending on a great deal of zeal and money to bring members of the government to the monarchist party[503]. But sometimes he thought he had bought them, and it happened that suspicious intermediaries pocketed the English gold and did not reappear.

The Directoire succeeded in having Wickham expelled from Switzerland in 1797, but Talbot soon replaced him. A credit of 1,250,000 francs, opened by Wickham to the royalist conspirators, had not been touched, to the great astonishment of England. Talbot was ordered to keep a million at their disposal. However, Poteratz, the diplomatic agent in Basle, continued to point out England's devious conduct towards the emigrants "whom she supported as long as they seemed useful to her designs and whom she sacrificed at Quiberon and in Germany"[504].

We have already drawn attention to the secret relationship between the Angle terre and our diplomacy. After Duroveray, the spy Baldwin officially joined the Foreign Office in 1791. Reinhardt's appointment under the Directoire was further proof

---

[502] E. DAUDET: *Les Bourbons et la Russie pendant l'émigration,* p. 62.

[503] Lebon: *L'Angleterre et l'émigration,* Preface, p. 25.

[504] *Foreign Affairs Archives,* Vienna, v. 365.

of "the ascendancy of the court in London over the direction of our diplomacy"[505]. Reinhardt, the son of a German pastor, was a talented man.

At the end of 1796, the British government advised the Vendeans and Bretons to keep quiet because it was preparing to hold elections in France by buying off the electorate[506]. But with Brottier's plot uncovered, the British agents advised their government to wait for events to unfold.

The changes made to the plans of the London cabinet under the Directoire did not prevent English influence from being exerted in Paris as successfully as it had been under the Convention. On one occasion, W. Pitt was secretly informed that "Talleyrand will be able to satisfy England if a sufficient sum is paid to Barras, Rewbell and their clique"[507]. On another occasion, it was Barras who was warned of the treason of a member of the government. "The plans and instructions of the Directoire were regularly communicated to Pitt"[508]. Thauvenay, agent and friend of the Count of Provence, informed d'Avaray that Lord Fitz-Gerald had criminal correspondence with the Directoire via Hamburg. -

Despite the laws against foreigners, English agents continued to swarm in Paris. For example, during Sidney Smith's famous escape in 1798, the false release order from the Ministry of the Navy was brought to the prison by the Scotsman Keith, from

---

[505] *Journal des hommes libres.* Fr. Masson: *Le département des Affaires étrangères pendant la Révolution,* p. 435.

[506] Lebon: *L'Angleterre et l'émigration,* p. 215.

[507] Holland Rose: *William Pitt,* p. 325.

[508] *Mémoires de Barras,* t. Il. (These memoirs are suspected by some authors of being apocryphal, and we quote them with reservations).

Harris House, commissioned by Boyd[509].

At the beginning of the Consulate, there were more than five thousand Englishmen in Paris, including Fox, Rolland, Fitz-Gerald and Spencer. As the Masonic lodges reopened, little by little the English began to flock to them. The Douai lodge alone had around a hundred British subjects[510].

Mr. L. Madelin, in an interesting lecture on Fouché[511], recently mentioned a network of English agencies covering the whole of Europe at the beginning of the Empire. The one in Bordeaux was still in existence in 1814, and when Wellington's English troops entered the city, Madelin tells us that they felt "at home" there.

In short, the aim of the foreign syndicate was achieved in France at the end of the Directoire: anarchy seemed to be definitive, the Catholic religion seemed to be destroyed, and France, ruined and disorganised, could no longer play a role in Europe.

But, with all its skill, the British government was unable to prevent the eighteenth Brumaire. It had not understood that by sowing anarchy it was preparing for dictatorship.

So, by getting rid of a peaceful adversary, England unwittingly contributed to bringing its most formidable enemy to the throne. The French people, who had revolted against the debonair authority of Louis XVI, happily accepted the tyranny of Napoleon I[er]. The demagogues became the flat courtiers of absolute power; and Europe was astonished to see the French

---

[509] DESMARETS: *Fifteen years on the force.*

[510] Most of them were prisoners of war, many of whom escaped thanks to the complicity of the French Freemasons.

[511] See the *Revue Française* of 14 June 1914.

nation rise from its ruins to fly from victory to victory.

SUPPORTING DOCUMENTS

Diplomatic documents relating to English action in France at the beginning of the Revolution

1ᵉʳ July 1789. —*Versailles:*

"... It is said publicly that England is bribing a considerable number of agents to stir up trouble..."

July 2nd. —... We persist in believing that it is the English alone who are stirring up the people...

July 3rd. —... The English are always suspected of having secret agents here who spread money...".[512]

13ᵗʰ August. —*Versailles: (M. de Montmorin to the French Minister in Berlin).*

"... The relations which exist between England and Prussia with regard to our internal affairs and the conference which was held at Potsdam strengthen our suspicions with regard to these two powers...

We cannot regard as slander what is said about their secret activities...

---

[512] *Archives des Affaires étrangères,* France, c. 1405. (Bulletins relating events from the opening of the Estates General to 15 July, sent by the Ministry to its diplomatic agents).

The King particularly recommends that you do everything in your power to find out what happened at the mysterious conference you are reporting on… We have reason to believe that Holland is taking part in the conspiracy of the courts in London and Berlin…".[513]

20th June. —*Berlin: (The Count of Esterno to M. de Montmorin.)*

… "All those who have access to the King of Prussia are sold to England. The Countess de Bruhl, wife of the Prince Royal's governor, is English and fanatical in her love for her country and her hatred for France… The court physician, a man of great wit, is English…".[514]

31st July. —*London: (M. de La Luzerne to the Minister.)*

… "The Duke of Leeds told me yesterday with an air of affected sorrow that he had been very distressed to read in a dispatch from the Duke of Dorset that a member of the States General had made it known that a neighbouring and rival nation appeared to have spread money among the people during the recent troubles… I have tried to persuade the Duke of Leeds that we are very reassured in this respect. But in truth, we cannot be too careful about the conduct of the English, which will certainly be as concealed as it is self-serving.

3rd August. —*Versailles: (M. de Montmorin to M. de La Luzerne).*

"The English have been violently suspected of spreading money among the people of Paris with the intention of stirring them up… I refrain from accusing the English ministry because

---

[513] *Foreign Affairs Archives.* Correspondence from Berlin, 1789.

[514] *Id.*

I have no proof against them and it is all the more difficult to acquire any as the police no longer exist, but what is certain is that the money has been spread with the greatest profusion among the soldiers as well as among the people… I beg you to turn your attention to this matter. As many Englishmen are returning home to escape the tumult, there may be some indiscreet people who could at least provide some clues."

10 August. —*Versailles:*

"I cannot recommend enough that you be extremely vigilant about the more or less active role that the English could play in our internal troubles"[515].

14 August. —*London:* (*M. de La Luzerne to M. de Montmorin.*)

The beginning of the letter sets out the conviction that the troubles in Paris were fomented by the Duke of Dorset:

… "I have no way of ascertaining whether he actually used as much money as is thought in Paris to debauch the troops and seduce the people. But what I can assure you is that as soon as the troops were ordered to approach Paris, and much before their arrival, Dorset assured his court that these troops would declare themselves for the people in preference to the King. This prophetic spirit makes us believe that he had extremely positive data and it is difficult to imagine how he could have acquired them if he had not himself entered into this infernal intrigue"[516]:

27th September 1789. —*London:* (*Barthélemy to M.*

---

[515] The end of the letter recommends monitoring relations between the French in London and the English Ministry.

[516] Correspondence from London, v. 570.

de Montmorin.)

... "The King of England hates France and would like our dissensions to avenge him for the war in America...".

23rd November. —*London: (M. de La Luzerne to M. de Montmorin.)*

... "I am trying to find out if, instead of talking to the English ministers about the affairs of the Netherlands, the Duc d'Orléans would not consult with them to stir up new troubles in France...,—but I do not believe that the King or Mr. Pitt support a Prince of the blood against the King. They have such a low opinion of the Duc d'Orléans, they believe him to be so unsuited to be the leader of a party, that they will certainly not mix their affairs with his. I cannot tell you how much the arrival of this Prince has given the English of all classes a bad opinion of him...

I have Laclos followed. He writes almost all day and receives many letters from France...

Calonne secretly sees the Duc d'Orléans and Duroveray...

26th November. —... Drumond is suspected of passing money to Hopp in Amsterdam in order to distribute money in Paris. "There are two Englishmen in Paris, one named Danton[517] and the other Parc, whom some people suspect of being the English government's most private agents...

Mlle Boulard, the Queen's chambermaid, is the Duke's spy.

---

[517] Opposite Danton's name, in the margin of the letter, are the words: "Président du district des Cordeliers". But this pencil note is in a different handwriting from those of M. de La Luzerne and M. de Montmorin. Doubting its authenticity, we quote it for the record.

The three people most attached to the Duke are Pitra, Paris and Abbé Fauchet. He also has great confidence in a man called Forth who was once sent to Paris by the English government. This Forth often sees Mr Pitt"[518].

A letter dated 18 December mentions Forth's departure, "probably for Paris".

I[st] January 1790. —... "The Duc d'Orléans, who spends the whole day at Mme de Buffon's, is invisible all day long. When he comes to see me: he talks to me about general affairs and never about his visits to the English minister, which I know are very frequent"...

January 3rd. —... "Forth returned very dissatisfied with his mission".

16th July. —The English were expecting serious disorder on 14 July... ". The Duke was strongly urged by the Prince of Wales to return to Paris on that date...".[519]

5th January 1791. —A letter from Barthélemy indicates England's fervent wish that the internal difficulties in France should worsen.

5 April. —M. de La Luzerne, following a conversation with the King of England, sums up his impression: "As long as we are in a situation where we cannot interfere in European affairs and above all cannot compete with England's trade, we will not be worried. But as soon as our Government regains strength and vigour, we can count on there being no intrigues, no open or devious means that these people will not employ to delay our progress and plunge us back, if they can, into the abyss in which

---

[518] Correspondence from London, v. 571 (encrypted dispatch).

[519] London Corr., v. 574.

we now find ourselves[520].

2nd September. —*Barthélemy to M. de Montmorin:*

"On the day of his departure, M. de Mercy said to me: "I have always been of the opinion that England had a hand in all the unfortunate divisions of your country. I am leaving here more convinced than ever of this sad truth, and that, against the interests of all the other powers which would like to see France regain its accustomed strength, England will continue to seek to undermine it surreptitiously in order to bring about its total ruin"…

M. de Mercy admits that there have been communications between the main powers of Europe on the subject of our affairs; concertation is impossible, especially because of England's secret views…

A foreign minister asked Lord Dover, Captain of the Royal Guards, what system he thought England would follow towards France: "At the time of our civil wars," he replied, "did France support the royalist party in our country?"[521] …

2nd December. —M. de Worontzof is irritated by the blindness of Russia and Spain, who do not see England's activities in France:

"It suits England that a long anarchy prevents the return of any government in France. If she has prevented the Landgrave of Hesse from giving troops to the French Princes, it is so that their party does not gain the upper hand solidly; but on the other hand she strongly encourages them to enter France with arms in

---

[520] London Corr. v. 577.

[521] London Corr., v. 579.

hand...".

30th December. —... " The King of England protests against the accusations of ill-intentioned people who take the liberty of attributing our troubles to England. Lord Granville repeats the same things... Pitt has had the skill to act only surreptitiously and secretly in all his endeavours against us...".[522]

Report by Saint-Just to the Committee of Public Safety.—25^e day of 1er ... month of year II:

... "The English seemed to think that the best way to wage war against a nascent Republic was rather to corrupt it than to fight it...".[523]

Pluviôse, year II (unsigned):

... "It is the English government that intrigues in Paris, murders the patriots and counterfeits the natural currency...".[524]

22nd March 1793. —... "One cannot doubt that there is in Paris a great number of English spies: I° Almost all the correspondents of the newspapers of London... 2° These characters whom one sees appearing and disappearing every week alternately in Paris and in London. The most remarkable is Captain Frazer, a Scotsman... 3° The three Irish superiors Walsh, Keruy and Mahew... 4° In the cafés you meet a large number of Englishmen whose remarks reveal, if not a formal plot against the system of liberty and equality, at least an ardent desire to see it destroyed...".

---

[522] London Corr., v. 579.

[523] London Corr., v. 588.

[524] *Id.*

May 1793. —*Ducher to the Minister of Foreign Affairs:*

... "For the last ten years the British Ministry has been pawning off in France the economists, this sect so much advocated by the English, Dutch and Genevan bankers, who are enriching themselves from the effects of its doctrine...".[525]

17 Floréal, year II. —*Buchot to the Minister: Amsterdam* — ... "The Committees must employ all their vigilance to prevent the plots directed from London against themselves and particularly against Robespierre. Pitt lavishes his gold on this...".

19 Thermidor, year II. —*Bucher, commissioner for foreign relations in Basle, to the minister:*

"The Pillnitz Convention and all subsequent arrangements are due to England's gold...".[526]

9 Vendémiaire, year III. —*Druy, secret agent, to the minister:*

London. —... "To make Pitt disappear or to make his head fall off, that must be the desire of all good Frenchmen. I will not urge you to take the smallest steps to destroy George's, as he will soon have none left...

"Pitt's top agents are in Paris...".

Year IV (unsigned). —*Report on the message of the British Cabinet:*

... "The insurrections in Lyon, Toulon and Marseilles, the civil wars, the continual raids by émigrés on our coasts, are all

---

[525] London Cor., v. 587.

[526] Berlin Corr., v. 213.

the work of Pitt… To fuel this internecine war, did he not have the audacity to set up a factory producing counterfeit assignats. I put the proof in front of you…".[527]

I5 December 1795. —*Poteratz to the minister: Basle.* —… "Remember the execrable conduct of the English government towards us since the beginning of the Revolution… fomenting by dint of intrigues and money trouble on all points of your interior, towards the émigrés whom it encouraged and supported as long as they seemed useful to its designs, whom it has sacrificed since, either at Quiberon or in Germany, and whom it will end up abandoning as soon as they cease to be necessary to it in order to harm us…; with the Chouans and the Vendée to whom it purposely provides only great promises and half measures… with the Chouans and the Vendée, to whom she purposely provides only grand promises and half-hearted support…".[528]

The condemnation of Louis XVI by Freemasonry

Several historians claim that the French Revolution and the death of Louis XVI were decided in Germany at the Masonic convents in Ingolstadt and Frankfurt.

Barruel's opinion on this point is confirmed by Cadet de Gassicourt, a former Freemason[529]. Several members of the

---

[527] London Corr., supplement, v. 15.

[528] Vienna Corr., v. 362.

[529] The tomb of Jacques Molai. See also: Deschamps: *Les sociétés secrètes,* t. II, p. 134 et seq. G. GAUTHEROT: *Histoire de l'Assemblée Constituante,* ch. II. De LANNOY: *La Révolution préparée par la Franc-maçonnerie,* p. 99 ff, etc.

sect have made formal statements in this regard, including MM. de Raymond, Bouligny and Jean Debry. They were said to have left Freemasonry on this occasion.

A recent controversy in *the Intermédiaire des chercheurs et des curieux* cast doubt on these assertions, based on the following fact: Messrs de Raymond, de Bouligny and Jean Debry are said to have remained Freemasons; therefore they did not leave with indignation the Secret Society which decided the death of the King of Sweden and the King of France. We conclude from this that all their accounts are suspect.

To this it is easy to reply that the fate of M. de Wal may have given them food for thought: M. de Wal allowed himself to divulge the Masonic projects whose violence he condemned. He disappeared shortly afterwards and his body was found buried in the forest of Fontainebleau. It was therefore very unwise to break ostensibly with Freemasonry. This is why Messrs de Raymond and de Bouligny did not speak until their deathbed.

Could they not also have assumed that by remaining members of the sect, they could steer it towards more moderate ideas and oppose violent decisions? By leaving, on the other hand, they lost all means of action and remained in the dark about the events that were being prepared behind the scenes.

Count Costa de Beauregard relates that the Count de Virieu withdrew from Freemasonry when he realised that the sect had three aims: "the ruin of religion, the dishonour of the queen and the death of the king". M. Gustave Bord objects that it is "*probably*" on the basis of Barruel's assertion that M. Costa de Beauregard gives this account, etc.". Why should it be according to Barruel's assertion? The de Virieu and Costa de Beauregard families were allies, and they lived in the same country. What wonder that the Costa family received the confidences of M. de Virieu! Moreover, Barruel was suspected of exaggeration but not of lying.

Another argument is the confession that Father Abel heard from his grandfather: the latter declared that he regretted his regicide vote at the Convent in Germany that decided on the death of Louis XVI. The objection is that this is verbal testimony given by a man of eighty. Since when do we no longer accept verbal testimony from men of eighty? We let them run a state and unleash war. If Mr Abel had been a child, would his family have divulged his testimony? They were in no way proud of the role he played. Besides, if we don't believe an old man's word, would his *written* testimony be any more valuable?

It seems to us, therefore, that the question remains open, and we would like to see the discussions of *the Intermédiaire des chercheurs et des curieux* continue.

As for Haugwitz's report, we believe it has not yet been refuted. And this is an official document from a former Freemason, confidant of the King of Prussia, affirming the condemnation of Louis XVI in 1784. As far as Gustav III is concerned, the Berlin legal archives contain (according to Messrs E. Faligant and Deschamps) proof of his condemnation by the Illuminati. The Count of Haugwitz, having retired from Freemasonry, stated that Louis XVI had also been condemned four or five years before the French Revolution. This testimony by M. de Haugwitz has never been denied. Charged by the King of Prussia with a report on secret societies, he wrote[530]: "The French Revolution and regicide were resolved by Freemasonry"[531].

---

[530] *Dorrows Danksehriften*, v. IV, pp. 211–221.

[531] It is worth recalling how the condemnation of Louis XVI was assessed by an illustrious man to whom the Republic has erected statues, Ernest Renan: "The murder of 21 January is the most hideous act of materialism, the most shameful profession ever made of ingratitude and baseness, of common villainy and oblivion of the past" (*La Monarchie Constitutionnelle en France*).

Foreigners on the list of members
of the Jacobin Club in 1790[532]

Alexandre (English).

Abbéma (Dutch).

Bidermann (Switzerland).

Bitaubé (Prussian).

Cabarru (Spanish).

Cavalcanti (Italian).

Clavière (Switzerland).

Cloots (Prussian).

Doppet (Italian).

Desfieux (Belgian).

Dufourny (Italian).

Erdmann (…).

Ferguson (English).

Fitz Gerald (English).

Fockedey (English).

Fougolis (...).

Gorani (Italian).

Halem (...).

From Hesse (German).

Keith (English).

---

[532] See Aulard: *Le Club des Jacobins,* etc.

Klispich (...).

La Harpe (Switzerland).

Loen (...).

Miles (English).

Oelsner (German).

Pio (Italian).

Schlabrendorf (Prussian).

Schsvatv (...).

Van den Yver (Dutch).

Van Praet (Belgian).

Arthur Young (English).

Suspected foreigners

Bacon.

Bolls.

Charke.

Coitam.

Hanker.

Hovelt.

Kauffmann.

Knapen.

Mendosa.

Mermilliod.

Oelsner.

Pulcherberg.

Raek.

Schluter.

Schnutz.

Sigri.

Stourm.

Walwein, etc.

CONGRESS OF PHILALÈTHES (1785–1787)

The Amis Réunis (Philalèthes) lodge, presided over by Savalette de Lange, played an important role in the preparations for the French Revolution. Its headquarters were at 37, rue de la Sourdière.

In 1785, the Philalethes convened a Congress in Paris under the pretext of discussing "Masonic science". The reports published by the *Monde maçonnique of* course omit any political discussions, and try to prove that for eighteen months the Philalèthes confined themselves to exchanging banal reflections[533]. The only interesting pages are the discussions with Cagliostro, who then presided over the mother lodge of the Egyptian rite at the Orient of Lyon, and proclaimed himself to be far superior to the other Freemasons. After being asked to accept the Philalethes' invitation, Cagliostro, in order to prove his power, promised to make them see God "and the intermediary spirits between God and men". However, in exchange for this miracle, Cagliostro demanded that the Philalethic archives be destroyed (we have not been able to find out for what purpose).

The Philalethes refused this sacrifice because they were concerned about their archives, and some of them wondered

---

[533] *The Masonic World*, v. XIV and XV.

whether Cagliostro might not by chance be an impostor. Nevertheless, a list of the members of the Convent was sent to Cagliostro so that he could choose those whom he deemed appropriate to initiate into the Egyptian rite; he was asked to give preference to foreigners.

In the end, everything worked out: the Philalethes did not burn their archives, and Cagliostro did not evoke God or angels in the rue de la Sourdière premises. But the Mother Lodge of the Egyptian Rite wrote that "the unknown Grand Master of true Masonry has set his eyes on the Philalethes. He has agreed to shine a ray of light into the darkness of their Temple". The reports are silent on this ray of light. The Masons to whom the proceedings of the Convent were communicated had to give a written undertaking on their honour to maintain absolute secrecy.

In the second year of the Congress, Doctor Stark wrote from Darmstadt that the next Convent would be more dangerous than useful, and advised the Philalethes to give their full confidence to Saint-Martin and Willermoz. This letter contradicts the official accounts, for if the Philalethes spoke only of Masonic science, it could not be *dangerous* to meet, and there was no reason to give full powers to two of them. Were Saint-Martin and Willermoz the official representatives of foreign Masonry, or was Doctor Stark expressing a personal opinion, it is difficult to find out. Whatever the case, the Congress broke up on 8 June 1787, and its mysterious work was continued by the Secret Committee (Willermoz, Mirabeau, Court de Gébelin, Bonneville and Chappe de la Heuzière).

Already published

OMNIA VERITAS
Omnia Veritas Ltd presents:
MYRON FAGAN
THE ILLUMINATI
AND THE
COUNCIL ON FOREIGN RELATIONS
The objective is to brainwash the people into accepting the phony peace bait to transform the United States into an enslaved unit of the United Nations' one-world government.
They have seized that power on orders from their masters of the great conspiracy
MYRON FAGAN
THE ILLUMINATI

OMNIA VERITAS
Omnia Veritas Ltd presents:
ARCHIBALD RAMSAY
THE NAMELESS WAR
THE JEWISH POWER AGAINST THE NATIONS
The author describes the anatomy of the machine of the Revolutionary International which today pursues the project of supranational world power, the age-old messianic dream of international Jewry...
Evidence of a centuries-old conspiracy against Europe and the whole of Christendom...
ARCHIBALD RAMSAY
THE NAMELESS WAR
THE JEWISH POWER AGAINST THE NATIONS

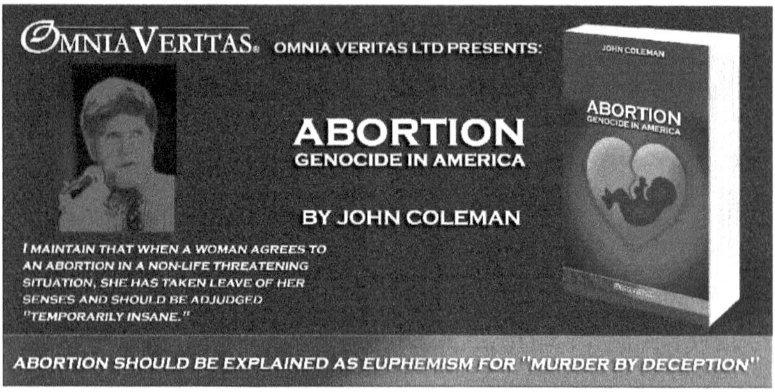
OMNIA VERITAS
OMNIA VERITAS LTD PRESENTS:
ABORTION
GENOCIDE IN AMERICA
BY JOHN COLEMAN
I MAINTAIN THAT WHEN A WOMAN AGREES TO AN ABORTION IN A NON-LIFE THREATENING SITUATION, SHE HAS TAKEN LEAVE OF HER SENSES AND SHOULD BE ADJUDGED "TEMPORARILY INSANE."
ABORTION SHOULD BE EXPLAINED AS EUPHEMISM FOR "MURDER BY DECEPTION"
JOHN COLEMAN
ABORTION
GENOCIDE IN AMERICA

OMNIA VERITAS
OMNIA VERITAS LTD PRESENTS:
BEYOND the CONSPIRACY
UNMASKING THE INVISIBLE WORLD GOVERNMENT
All great historical events are planned in secret by men who surround themselves with total discretion.
by John Coleman
JOHN COLEMAN
Highly organized groups always have the advantage over citizens

OMNIA VERITAS
OMNIA VERITAS LTD PRESENTS:
THE CLUB OF ROME
THE THINK TANK OF THE NEW WORLD ORDER
The many tragic and explosive events of the 20th century didn't happen by themselves, but were planned according to a well-established pattern...
BY JOHN COLEMAN
Who were the planners and creators of these major events?

OMNIA VERITAS
OMNIA VERITAS LTD PRESENTS:
JOHN COLEMAN
DIPLOMACY BY DECEPTION
BY JOHN COLEMAN
DIPLOMACY BY DECEPTION
AN ACCOUNT OF THE TREASONOUS CONDUCT BY THE GOVERNMENTS OF BRITAIN AND THE UNITED STATES
The story of the creation of the United Nations is a classic case of diplomacy by deception

The drug trade cannot be eradicated because its directors will not allow the world's most lucrative market to be taken away from them...

DRUG WAR against AMERICA

BY JOHN COLEMAN

The real promoters of this cursed trade are the "elites" of this world.

In the 21st century, Freemasonry has become less a secret society than a "society of secrets".

FREEMASONRY from A to Z

by John Coleman

This book explains what masonry is

THE ROTHSCHILD DYNASTY

by John Coleman

Historical events are often caused by a "hidden hand"...

OMNIA VERITAS

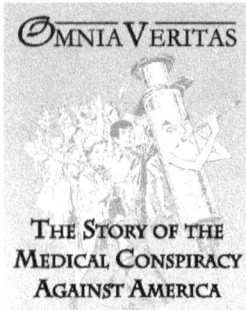

Omnia Veritas Ltd presents:

MURDER BY INJECTION

by

EUSTACE MULLINS

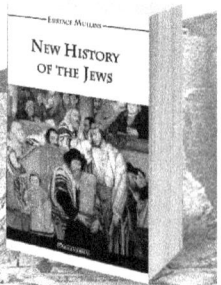

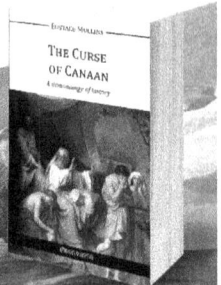

THE STORY OF THE MEDICAL CONSPIRACY AGAINST AMERICA

The cynicism and malice of these conspirators is something beyond the imagination of most Americans.

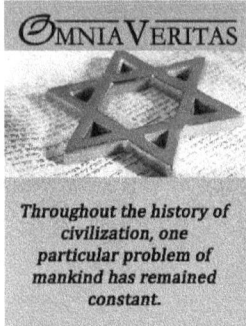

OMNIA VERITAS

Omnia Veritas Ltd presents:

NEW HISTORY OF THE JEWS

by

EUSTACE MULLINS

Throughout the history of civilization, one particular problem of mankind has remained constant.

Only one people bas irritated its host nations in every part of the civilized world

OMNIA VERITAS

Omnia Veritas Ltd presents:

THE CURSE OF CANAAN

A demonology of history

by

EUSTACE MULLINS

Liberalism, more popularly known as secular humanism, can be traced in an unbroken line all the way back to the Biblical "Curse of Canaan."

Humanism is the logical result of the demonology of history

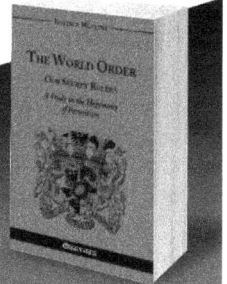

OMNIA VERITAS
OMNIA VERITAS LTD PRESENTS:
ROGER GARAUDY
THE FOUNDING MYTHS
OF ISRAELI POLITICS
ROGER GARAUDY
THE FOUNDING MYTHS OF ISRAELI POLITICS
Who is guilty? Who commits the crime or who denounces it?

OMNIA VERITAS
MK ULTRA
Ritual Abuse and Mind Control
Tools of domination for
the nameless religion
For the first time, a book
attempts to explore the
complex subjects of traumatic
ritual abuse and the mind
control that results from it...
MK ULTRA
How is it possible to mentally program a human being?

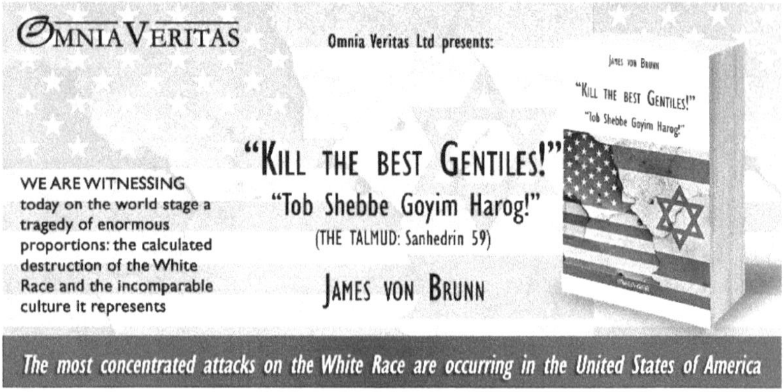
OMNIA VERITAS
Omnia Veritas Ltd presents:
WE ARE WITNESSING
today on the world stage a
tragedy of enormous
proportions: the calculated
destruction of the White
Race and the incomparable
culture it represents
"KILL THE BEST GENTILES!"
"Tob Shebbe Goyim Harog!"
(THE TALMUD: Sanhedrin 59)
JAMES VON BRUNN
"KILL THE BEST GENTILES!"
The most concentrated attacks on the White Race are occurring in the United States of America

ΘMNIA VERITAS. Omnia Veritas Ltd presents:

FREDERICK SODDY

FREDERICK SODDY

THE ROLE OF MONEY

THE ROLE OF MONEY
WHAT IT SHOULD BE CONTRASTED
WITH WHAT IT HAS BECOME

WHAT IT SHOULD BE CONTRASTED WITH WHAT IT HAS BECOME

This book attempts to clear up the mystery of money in its social aspect

This, surely, is what the public really wants to know about money

ΘMNIA VERITAS. Omnia Veritas Ltd presents:

FREDERICK SODDY

FREDERICK SODDY

WEALTH, VIRTUAL WEALTH AND DEBT

WEALTH, VIRTUAL WEALTH AND DEBT

THE SOLUTION OF THE ECONOMIC PARADOX

The most powerful tyranny and the most universal conspiracy against the economic freedom of individuals and the autonomy of nations world has yet known.

THE SOLUTION OF THE ECONOMIC PARADOX

The public are most carefully shielded from any real knowledge...

ΘMNIA VERITAS. Omnia Veritas Ltd presents:

EUSTACE MULLINS

An exclusive and unpublished work of EUSTACE MULLINS

BLOOD AND GOLD
HISTORY OF THE COUNCIL ON FOREIGN RELATIONS

BLOOD AND GOLD
HISTORY OF THE COUNCIL OF FOREIGN RELATIONS

The CFR, founded by internationalists and banking interests, has played a significant role in shaping US foreign policy

Revolutions are not made by the middle class, but by the oligarchy at the top

www.ingramcontent.com/pod-product-compliance
Lightning Source LLC
Chambersburg PA
CBHW070906270326
41927CB00011B/2475